Comment

MW01293959

Matthew Henry

Revelation Introduction

An Exposition, with Practical Observations, of The Revelation of St. John the Divine

It ought to be no prejudice to the credit and authority of this book that it has been rejected by men of corrupt minds, such as Cerdon and Marcion, and doubted of by men of a better character; for this has been the lot of other parts of holy writ, and of the divine Author of the scripture himself. The image and superscription of this book are truly sacred and divine, and the matter of it agreeable with other prophetical books, particularly Ezekiel and Daniel; the church of God has generally received it, and found good counsel and great comfort in it. From the beginning, the church of God has been blessed with prophecy. That glorious prediction of breaking the serpent's head was the stay and support of the patriarchal age; and the many prophecies there were concerning the Messiah to come were the gospel of the Old Testament. Christ himself prophesied of the destruction of Jerusalem; and, about the time in which that was accomplished, he entrusted the apostle John with this book of revelation, to deliver it to the church as a prediction of the most important events that should happen to it to the end of time, for the support of the faith of his people and the direction of their hope. It is called the Revelation, because God therein discovers those things which could never have been sifted out by the reasonings of human understanding, those deep things of God which no man knows, but the Spirit of God, and those to whom he reveals them.

Revelation Chapter 1

This chapter is a general preface to the whole book, and contains, I. An inscription, declaring the original and the design of it (Rev 1:1, Rev 1:2). II. The apostolic benediction pronounced on all those who shall pay a due regard to the contents of this book (Rev 1:3-8). III. A glorious vision or appearance of the Lord Jesus Christ to the apostle John, when he delivered to him this revelation (Rev 1:9 to the end).

Revelation 1:1

Here we have,

I. What we may call the pedigree of this book. 1. It is the revelation of Jesus Christ. The whole Bible is so; for all revelation comes through Christ and all centres in him; and especially in these last days God has spoken to us by his Son, and concerning his Son. Christ, as the king of his church, has been pleased thus far to let his church know by what rules and methods he will proceed in his government; and, as the prophet of the church, he has made known to us the things that shall be hereafter. 2. It is a revelation which God gave unto Christ. Though Christ is himself God, and as such has light and life in himself, yet, as he sustains the office of Mediator between God and man, he receives his instructions from the Father. The human nature of Christ, though endowed with the greatest sagacity, judgment, and penetration, could not, in a way of reason, discover these great events, which not being produced by natural causes, but wholly depending upon the will of God, could be the object only of divine prescience, and must come to a created mind only by revelation. Our Lord Jesus is the great trustee of divine revelation; it is to him that we owe the knowledge we have of what we are to expect from God and what he expects from us. 3. This revelation Christ sent and signified by his angel. Observe here the admirable order of divine revelation. God gave it to Christ, and Christ employed an angel to communicate it to the churches. The angels are God's messengers; they are ministering spirits to the heirs of salvation. They are Christ's servants: principalities and powers are subject to him; all the angels of God are obliged to worship him. 4. The angels signified it to the apostle John. As the angels are the messengers of Christ, the ministers are the messengers of the churches; what they receive from heaven, they are to communicate to the churches. John was the apostle chosen for this service. Some think he was the only one surviving, the rest having sealed their testimony with their blood. This was to be the last book of divine revelation; and therefore notified to the church by the last of the apostles. John was the beloved disciple. He was, under the New Testament, as the prophet Daniel under the Old, a man greatly beloved. He was the servant of Christ; he was an apostle, an evangelist, and a prophet; he served Christ in all the three extraordinary offices of the church. James was an apostle, but not a prophet, nor an evangelist; Matthew was an apostle and evangelist, but not a prophet; Luke was an evangelist, but neither a prophet nor an apostle; but John was all three; and so Christ calls him in an eminent sense his servant John. 5. John was to deliver this revelation to the church, to all his servants. For the revelation was not designed for the use of Christ's extraordinary servants the ministers only, but for all his servants, the members of the church; they have all a right to the oracles of God, and all have their concern in them.

II. Here we have the subject-matter of this revelation, namely, the things that must shortly come to pass. The evangelists give us an account of the things that are past; prophecy gives us an account of things to come. These future events are shown, not in the clearest light in which God could have set them, but in such a light as he saw most proper, and which would best answer his wise and holy purposes. Had they been as clearly foretold in all their circumstances as God could have revealed them, the prediction might have prevented the accomplishment; but they are foretold more darkly, to beget in us a veneration for the scripture, and to engage our attention and excite our enquiry. We have in this revelation a general idea of the methods of divine providence and government in and about the church, and many good lessons may be learned hereby. These events (it is said) were such as should come to pass not only surely, but shortly; that is, they would begin to come to pass very shortly, and the whole would be accomplished in a short time. For now the last ages of the world had come.

III. Here is an attestation of the prophecy, Rev 1:2. It was signified to John, who bore record of the word of God, and of the testimony of Jesus Christ, and of all things that he saw. It is observable that the historical books of the Old Testament have not always the name of the historian prefixed to them, as in the books of Judges, Kings, Chronicles; but in the prophetical books the name is always prefixed, as Isaiah, Jeremiah, etc. So in the New Testament, though John did not prefix his name to his first epistle, yet he does to this prophecy, as ready to vouch and answer for the truth of it; and he gives us not only his name, but his office. He was one who bore record of the word of God in general, and of the testimony of Jesus in particular, and of all things that he saw; he was an eye-witness, and he concealed nothing that he saw. Nothing recorded in this revelation was his own invention or imagination; but all was the record of God and the testimony of Jesus; and, as he added nothing to it, so he kept back no part of the counsels of God.

Revelation 1:3

We have here an apostolic benediction on those who should give a due regard to this divine revelation; and this benediction is given more generally and more especially.

I. More generally, to all who either read or hear the words of the prophecy. This blessing seems to be pronounced with a design to encourage us to study this book, and not be weary of looking into it upon account of the obscurity of many things in it; it will repay the labour of the careful and attentive reader. Observe, 1. It is a blessed privilege to enjoy the oracles of God. This was one of the principal advantages the Jews had above the Gentiles. 2. It is a blessed thing to study the scriptures; those are well employed who search the scriptures. 3. It is a privilege not only to read the scriptures ourselves, but to hear them read by others, who are qualified to give us the sense of what they read and to lead us into an understanding of them. 4. It is not sufficient to our blessedness that we read and hear the scriptures, but we must keep the things that are written; we must keep them in our memories, in our minds, in our affections, and in practice, and we shall be blessed in the deed. 5. The nearer we come to the accomplishment of the scriptures, the greater regard we shall give to them. The time is at hand, and we should be so much the more attentive as we see the day approaching.

II. The apostolic benediction is pronounced more especially and particularly to the seven Asian churches, Rev 1:4. These seven churches are named in Rev 1:11, and distinct messages sent to each of them respectively in the chapters following. The apostolic blessing is more expressly directed to these because they were nearest to him, who was now in the isle of Patmos, and perhaps he had the peculiar care of them, and superintendency over them, not excluding any of the rest of the apostles, if any of them were now living. Here observe,

1. What the blessing is which he pronounces on all the faithful in these churches: Grace and peace, holiness and comfort. Grace, that is, the good-will of God towards us and his good work in us; and peace, that is, the sweet evidence and assurance of this grace. There can be no true peace where there is not true grace; and, where grace goes before, peace will follow.

2. Whence this blessing is to come. In whose name does the apostle bless the churches? In the name of God, of the whole Trinity; for this is an act of adoration, and God only is the proper object of it; his ministers must bless the people in no name but his alone. And here, (1.) The Father is first named: God the Father, which may be taken either essentially, for God as God, or personally, for the first person in the ever-blessed Trinity, the God and Father of our Lord Jesus Christ; and he is described as the Jehovah who is, and who was, and who is to come, eternal, unchangeable, the same to the Old Testament church which was, and to the New Testament church which is, and who will be the same to the church triumphant which is to come. (2.) The Holy Spirit, called the seven spirits, not seven in number, nor in nature, but the infinite perfect Spirit of God, in whom there is a diversity of gifts and operations. He is before the throne; for, as God made, so he governs, all things by his Spirit. (3.) The Lord Jesus Christ. He mentions him after the Spirit, because he intended to enlarge more upon the person of Christ, as God manifested in the flesh, whom he had seen dwelling on earth before, and now saw again in a glorious form. Observe the particular account we have here of Christ, Rev 1:5. [1.] He is the faithful witness; he was from eternity a witness to all the counsels of God (Joh 1:18), and he was in time a faithful witness to the revealed will of God, who has now spoken to us by his Son; upon his testimony we may safely depend, for he is a faithful witness, cannot be deceived and cannot deceive us. [2.] He is the first-begotten or first-born from the dead, or the first parent and head of the resurrection, the only one who raised himself by his own power, and who will by the same power raise up his people from their graves to everlasting honour; for he has begotten them again to a lively hope by his resurrection from the dead. [3.] He is the prince of the kings of the earth; from him they have their authority; by him their power is limited and their wrath restrained; by him their counsels are over-ruled, and to him they are accountable. This is good news to the church, and it is good evidence of the Godhead of Christ, who is King of kings and Lord of lords. [4.] He is the great friend of his church and people, one who has done great things for them, and this out of pure disinterested affection. He has loved them, and, in pursuance of that everlasting love, he has, First, Washed them from their sins in his own blood. Sins leave a stain upon the soul, a stain of guilt and of pollution. Nothing can fetch out this stain but the blood of Christ; and, rather than it should not be washed out, Christ was willing to shed his own blood, to purchase pardon and purity for them. Secondly, He has made them kings and priests to God and his Father. Having justified and sanctified them, he makes them kings to his Father; that is, in his Father's account, with his approbation, and for his glory. As kings, they govern their own spirits, conquer Satan, have power and prevalency with God in prayer, and shall judge the world. He hath made them priests, given them access to God, enabled them to enter into the holiest and to offer spiritual and acceptable sacrifices, and has given them an unction suitable to this character;

and for these high honours and favours they are bound to ascribe to him dominion and glory for ever. [5.] He will be the Judge of the world: Behold, he cometh, and every eye shall see him, Rev 1:7. This book, the Revelation, begins and ends with a prediction of the second coming of the Lord Jesus Christ. We should set ourselves to meditate frequently upon the second coming of Christ, and keep it in the eye of our faith and expectation. John speaks as if he saw that day: "Behold, he cometh, as sure as if you beheld him with your eyes. He cometh with clouds, which are his chariot and pavilion. He will come publicly: Every eye shall see him, the eye of his people, the eye of his enemies, every eye, yours and mine." He shall come, to the terror of those who have pierced him and have not repented and of all who have wounded and crucified him afresh by their apostasy from him, and to the astonishment of the pagan world. For he comes to take vengeance on those who know not God, as well as on those that obey not the gospel of Christ. [6.] This account of Christ is ratified and confirmed by himself, Rev 1:8. Here our Lord Jesus justly challenges the same honour and power that is ascribed to the Father, Rev 1:4. He is the beginning and the end; all things are from him and for him; he is the Almighty; he is the same eternal and unchangeable one. And surely whoever presumes to blot out one character of this name of Christ deserves to have his name blotted out of the book of life. Those that honour him he will honour; but those who despise him shall be lightly esteemed.

Revelation 1:9

We have now come to that glorious vision which the apostle had of the Lord Jesus Christ, when he came to deliver this revelation to him, where observe,

I. The account given of the person who was favoured with this vision. He describes himself, 1. By his present state and condition. He was the brother and companion of these churches in tribulation, and in the kingdom and patience of Christ. He was, at their time, as the rest of true Christians were, a persecuted man, banished, and perhaps imprisoned, for his adherence to Christ. He was their brother, though an apostle; he seems to value himself upon his relation to the church, rather than his authority in it: Judas Iscariot may be an apostle, but not a brother in the family of God. He was their companion: the children of God should choose communion and society with each other. He was their companion in tribulation: the persecuted servants of God did not suffer alone, the same trials are accomplished in others. He was their companion in patience, not only a sharer with them in suffering circumstances, but in suffering graces: if we have the patience of the saints, we should not grudge to meet with their trials. He was their brother and companion in the patience of the kingdom of Christ, a sufferer for Christ's cause, for asserting his kingly power over the church and the world, and for adhering to it against all who would usurp upon it. By this account he gives of his present state, he acknowledges his engagements to sympathize with them, and to endeavour to give them counsel and comfort, and bespeaks their more careful attention to what he had to say to them from Christ their common Lord. 2. By the place where he was when he was favoured with this vision: he was in the isle Patmos. He does not say who banished him thither. It becomes Christians to speak sparingly and modestly of their own sufferings. Patmos is said to be an island in the Aegean Sea, One of those called Cyclades, and was about thirty-five miles in compass; but under this confinement it was the apostle's comfort that he did not suffer as an evil-doer, but that it was for the testimony of Jesus, for bearing witness to Christ as the Immanuel, the Saviour. This was a cause worth suffering for; and the Spirit of glory and of God rested upon this persecuted apostle. 3. The day and time in which he had this vision: it was the Lord's day, the day which Christ had separated and set apart for himself, as the eucharist is called the Lord's supper. Surely this can be no other than the Christian sabbath, the first day of the week, to be observed in remembrance of the resurrection of Christ. Let us who call him our Lord honour him on his own day, the day which the Lord hath made and in which we ought to rejoice. 4. The frame that his soul was in at this time: He was in the Spirit. He was not only in a rapture when he received the vision, but before he received it; he was in a serious, heavenly, spiritual frame, under the blessed gracious influences of the Spirit of God. God usually prepares the souls of his people for uncommon manifestations of himself, by the quickening sanctifying influences of his good Spirit. Those who would enjoy communion with God on the Lord's day must endeavour to abstract their thoughts and affections from flesh and fleshly things, and be wholly taken up with things of a spiritual nature.

II. The apostle gives an account of what he heard when thus in the Spirit. An alarm was given as with the sound of a trumpet, and then he heard a voice, the voice of Christ applying to himself the character before given, the first and the last, and commanding the apostle to commit to writing the things that were now to be revealed to him, and to send it immediately to the seven Asian churches, whose names are mentioned. Thus our Lord Jesus, the captain of our salvation, gave the apostle notice of his glorious appearance, as with the sound of a trumpet.

III. We have also an account of what he saw. He turned to see the voice, whose it was and whence it came; and then a wonderful scene of vision opened itself to him.

1. He saw a representation of the church under the emblem of seven golden candlesticks, as it is explained in the last verse of the chapter. The churches are compared to candlesticks, because they hold forth the light of the gospel to advantage. The churches are not candles: Christ only is our light, and his gospel our lamp; but they receive their light from Christ and the gospel, and hold it forth to others. They are golden candlesticks, for they should be precious and pure, comparable to fine gold; not only the ministers, but the members of the churches ought to be such; their light should so shine before men as to engage others to give glory to God.

2. He saw a representation of the Lord Jesus Christ in the midst of the golden candlesticks; for he has promised to be with his churches always to the end of the world, filling them with light, and life, and love, for he is the very animating informing soul of the church. And here we observe,

(1.) The glorious form in which Christ appeared in several particulars. [1.] He was clothed with a garment down to the foot, a princely and priestly robe, denoting righteousness and honour. [2.] He was girt about with a golden girdle, the breast-plate of the high priest, on which the names of his people are engraven; he was ready girt to do all the work of a Redeemer. [3.] His head and hairs were white like wool or snow. He was the Ancient of days; his hoary head was no sign of decay, but was indeed a crown of glory. [4.] His eyes were as a flame of fire, piercing and penetrating into the very hearts and reins of men, scattering terrors among his adversaries. [5.] His feet were like unto fine burning brass, strong and stedfast, supporting his own interest, subduing his enemies, treading them to powder. [6.] His voice was as the sound of many waters, of many rivers falling in together. He can and will make himself heard to those who are afar off as well as to those who are near. His gospel is a profluent and mighty stream, fed by the upper springs of infinite wisdom and knowledge. [7.] He had in his right hand seven stars, that is, the ministers of the seven churches, who are under his direction, have all their light and influence from him, and are secured and preserved by him. [8.] Out of his mouth went a two-edged sword, his word, which both wounds and heals, strikes at sin on the right hand and on the left, [9.] His countenance was as the sun shining, its strength too bright and dazzling for mortal eyes to behold.

(2.) The impression this appearance of Christ made upon the apostle John (Rev 1:17): He fell at the feet of Christ as dead; he was overpowered with the greatness of the lustre and glory in which Christ appeared, though he had been so familiar with him before. How well is it for us that God speaks to us by men like ourselves, whose terrors shall not make us afraid, for none can see the face of God and live!

(3.) The condescending goodness of the Lord Jesus to his disciple: He laid his hand upon him, Rev 1:17. He raised him up; he did not plead against him with his great power, but he put strength into him, he spoke kind words to him. [1.] Words of comfort and encouragement: Fear not. He commanded away the slavish fears of his disciple. [2.] Words of instruction, telling him particularly who he was that thus appeared to him. And here he acquaints him, First, with his divine nature: The first and the last. Secondly, With his former sufferings: I was dead; the very same that his disciples saw upon the cross dying for the sins of men. Thirdly, With his resurrection and life: "I live, and am alive for evermore, have conquered death and opened the grave, and am partaker of an endless life." Fourthly, With his office and authority: I have the keys of hell and of death, a sovereign dominion in and over the invisible world, opening and none can shut, shutting so that none can open, opening the gates of death when he pleases and the gates of the eternal world, of happiness or misery, as the Judge of all, from whose sentence there lies no appeal. Fifthly, With his will and pleasure: Write the things which thou hast seen, and the things which are, and which shall be hereafter. Sixthly, With the meaning of the seven stars, that they are the ministers of the churches; and of the seven candlesticks, that they are the seven churches, to whom Christ would now send by him particular and proper messages.

Revelation Chapter 2

The apostle John, having in the foregoing chapter written the things which he had seen, now proceeds to write the things that are, according to the command of God (Rev 1:19), that is, the present state of the seven churches of Asia, with which he had a particular acquaintance, and for which he had a tender concern. He was directed to write to every one of them according to their present state and circumstances, and to inscribe every letter to the angel of that church, to the minister or rather ministry of that church, called angels because they are the messengers of God to mankind. In this chapter we have, I. The message sent to Ephesus (Rev 2:1-7). II. To Smyrna (Rev 2:8-11). III. To Pergamos (Rev 2:12-17). IV. To Thyatira (Rev 2:18, etc.).

Revelation 2:1

We have here,

I. The inscription, where observe, 1. To whom the first of these epistles is directed: To the church of Ephesus, a famous church planted by the apostle Paul (Acts 19), and afterwards watered and governed by John, who had his residence very much there. We can hardly think that Timothy was the angel, or sole pastor and bishop, of this church at this time,-that he who was of a very excellent spirit, and naturally cared for the good state of the souls of the people, should become so remiss as to deserve the rebukes given to the ministry of this church. Observe, 2. From whom this epistle to Ephesus was sent; and here we have one of those titles that were given to Christ in his appearance to John in the chapter foregoing: He that holds the seven stars in his right hand, and walks in the midst of the seven golden candlesticks, Rev 1:13, Rev 1:16. This title consists of two parts:-(1.) He that holds the stars in his right hand. The ministers of Christ are under his special care and protection. It is the honour of God that he knows the number of the stars, calls them by their names, binds the sweet influences of Pleiades and looses the bands of Orion; and it is the honour of the Lord Jesus Christ that the ministers of the gospel, who are greater blessings to the church than the stars are to the world, are in his hand. He directs all their motions; he disposes of them into their several orbs; he fills them with light and influence; he supports them, or else they would soon be falling stars; they are instruments in his hand, and all the good they do is done by his hand with them. (2.) He walks in the midst of the golden candlesticks. This intimates his relation to his churches, as the other his relation to his ministers. Christ is in an intimate manner present and conversant with his churches; he knows and observes their state; he takes pleasure in them, as a man does to walk in his garden. Though Christ is in heaven, he walks in the midst of his churches on earth, observing what is amiss in them and what it is that they want. This is a great encouragement to those who have the care of the churches, that the Lord Jesus has graven them upon the palms of his hands.

II. The contents of the epistle, in which, as in most of those that follow, we have,

1. The commendation Christ gave this church, ministers and members, which he always brings in

by declaring that he knows their works, and therefore both his commendation and reprehension are to be strictly regarded; for he does not in either speak at a venture: he knows what he says. Now the church of Ephesus is commended, (1.) For their diligence in duty: I know thy works, and thy labour,Rev 2:2. This may more immediately relate to the ministry of this church, which had been laborious and diligent. Dignity calls for duty. Those that are stars in Christ's hand had need to be always in motion, dispensing light to all about them. For my name's sake thou hast laboured, and hast not fainted, Rev 2:3. Christ keeps an account of every day's work, and every hour's work, his servants do for him, and their labour shall not be in vain in the Lord. (2.) For their patience in suffering: Thy labour and thy patience, Rev 2:2. It is not enough that we be diligent, but we must be patient, and endure hardness as good soldiers of Christ. Ministers must have and exercise great patience, and no Christian can be without it. There must be bearing patience, to endure the injuries of men and the rebukes of Providence; and there must be waiting patience, that, when they have done the will of God, they may receive the promise: Thou hast borne, and hast patience, Rev 2:3. We shall meet with such difficulties in our way and work as require patience to go on and finish well. (3.) For their zeal against what was evil: Thou canst not bear those that are evil, Rev 2:2. It consists very well with Christian patience not to dispense with sin, much less allow it; though we must show all meekness to men, yet we must show a just zeal against their sins. This their zeal was the more to be commended because it was according to knowledge, a discreet zeal upon a previous trial made of the pretences, practices, and tenets of evil men: Thou hast tried those that say they are apostles and are not, and hast found them liars. True zeal proceeds with discretion; none should be cast off till they be tried. Some had risen up in this church that pretended to be not ordinary ministers, but apostles; and their pretensions had been examined but found to be vain and false. Those that impartially search after truth may come to the knowledge of it.

2. The rebuke given to this church: Nevertheless, I have somewhat against thee,Rev 2:4. Those that have much good in them may have something much amiss in them, and our Lord Jesus, as an impartial Master and Judge, takes notice of both; though he first observes what is good, and is most ready to mention this, yet he also observes what is amiss, and will faithfully reprove them for it. The sin that Christ charged this church with was their decay and declension in holy love and zeal: Thou hast left thy first love; not left and forsaken the object of it, but lost the fervent degree of it that at first appeared. Observe, (1.) The first affections of men towards Christ, and holiness, and heaven, are usually lively and warm. God remembered the love of Israel's espousals, when she would follow him withersoever he went. (2.) These lively affections will abate and cool if great care be not taken, and diligence used, to preserve them in constant exercise. (3.) Christ is grieved and displeased with his people when he sees them grow remiss and cold towards him, and he will one way or other make them sensible that he does not take it well from them.

3. The advice and counsel given them from Christ: Remember therefore whence thou hast fallen, and repent, etc. (1.) Those that have lost their first love must remember whence they have fallen; they must compare their present with their former state, and consider how much better it was with them then than now, how much peace, strength, purity, and pleasure they have lost, by leaving their first love,-how much more comfortably they could lie down and sleep at night,-how much more cheerfully they could awake in the morning,-how much better they could bear afflictions, and how much more becomingly they could enjoy the favours of Providence,-how

much easier the thoughts of death were to them, and how much stronger their desires and hopes of heaven. (2.) They must repent. They must be inwardly grieved and ashamed for their sinful declension; they must blame themselves, and shame themselves, for it, and humbly confess it in the sight of God, and judge and condemn themselves for it. (3.) They must return and do their first works. They must as it were begin again, go back step by step, till they come to the place where they took the first false step; they must endeavour to revive and recover their first zeal, tenderness, and seriousness, and must pray as earnestly, and watch as diligently, as they did when they first set out in the ways of God.

4. This good advice is enforced and urged, (1.) By a severe threatening, if it should be neglected: I will come unto thee quickly, and remove thy candlestick out of its place. If the presence of Christ's grace and Spirit be slighted, we may expect the presence of his displeasure. He will come in a way of judgment, and that suddenly and surprisingly, upon impenitent churches and sinners; he will unchurch them, take away his gospel, his ministers, and his ordinances from them, and what will the churches or the angels of the churches do when the gospel is removed? (2.) By an encouraging mention that is made of what was yet good among them: This thou hast, that thou hatest the deeds of the Nicolaitans, which I also hate, Rev 2:6. "Though thou hast declined in thy love to what is good, yet thou retainest thy hatred to what is evil, especially to what is grossly so." The Nicolaitans were a loose sect who sheltered themselves under the name of Christianity. They held hateful doctrines, and they were guilty of hateful deeds, hateful to Christ and to all true Christians; and it is mentioned to the praise of the church of Ephesus that they had a just zeal and abhorrence of those wicked doctrines and practices. An indifference of spirit between truth and error, good and evil, may be called charity and meekness, but it is not pleasing to Christ. Our Saviour subjoins this kind commendation to his severe threatening, to make the advice more effectual.

III. We have the conclusion of this epistle, in which, as in those that follow, we have,

1. A call to attention: He that hath an ear, let him hear what the Spirit saith unto the churches. Observe, (1.) What is written in the scriptures is spoken by the Spirit of God. (2.) What is said to one church concerns all the churches, in every place and age. (3.) We can never employ our faculty of hearing better than in hearkening to the word of God: and we deserve to lose it if we do not employ it to this purpose. Those who will not hear the call of God now will wish at length they had never had a capacity of hearing any thing at all.

2. A promise of great mercy to those who overcome. The Christian life is a warfare against sin, Satan, the world, and the flesh. It is not enough that we engage in this warfare, but we must pursue it to the end, we must never yield to our spiritual enemies, but fight the good fight, till we gain the victory, as all persevering Christians shall do; and the warfare and victory shall have a glorious triumph and reward. That which is here promised to the victors is that they shall eat of the tree of life which is in the midst of the paradise of God. They shall have that perfection of holiness, and that confirmation therein, which Adam would have had if he had gone well through the course of his trial: he would then have eaten of the tree of life which was in the midst of paradise, and this would have been the sacrament of confirmation to him in his holy and happy state; so all who persevere in their Christian trial and warfare shall derive from Christ, as the tree of life, perfection and confirmation in holiness and happiness in the paradise of God; not in the

earthly paradise, but the heavenly, Rev 22:1,Rev 22:2.

Revelation 2:8

We now proceed to the second epistle sent to another of the Asian churches, where, as before, observe,

I. The preface or inscription in both parts. 1. The superscription, telling us to whom it was more expressly and immediately directed: To the angel of the church in Smyrna, a place well known at this day by our merchants, a city of great trade and wealth, perhaps the only city of all the seven that is still known by the same name, now however no longer distinguished for its Christian church being overrun by Mahomedism. 2. The subscription, containing another of the glorious titles of our Lord Jesus, the first and the last, he that was dead and is alive, taken out of Rev 1:17, Rev 1:18. (1.) Jesus Christ is the first and the last. It is but a little scantling of time that is allowed to us in this world, but our Redeemer is the first and the last. He is the first, for by him all things were made, and he was before all things with God and was God himself. he is the last, for all things are made for him, and he will be the Judge of all. This surely is the title of God, from everlasting and to everlasting, and it is the title of one that is an unchangeable Mediator between God and man, Jesus, the same yesterday, today, and for ever. He was the first, for by him the foundation of the church was laid in the patriarchal state; and he is the last, for by him the top-stone will be brought forth and laid in the end of time. (2.) He was dead and is alive. He was dead, and died for our sins; he is alive, for he rose again for our justification, and he ever lives to make intercession for us. He was dead, and by dying purchased salvation for us; he is alive, and by his life applies this salvation to us. And if, when we were enemies, we were reconciled by his death, much more, being reconciled, we shall be saved by his life. His death we commemorate every sacrament day; his resurrection and life every sabbath day.

II. The subject-matter of this epistle to Smyrna, where, after the common declaration of Christ's omniscience, and the perfect cognizance he has of all the works of men and especially of his churches, he takes notice,

1. Of the improvement they had made in their spiritual state. This comes in in a short parentheses; yet it is very emphatic: But thou art rich (Rev 2:10), poor in temporals, but rich in spirituals-poor in spirit, and yet rich in grace. Their spiritual riches are set off by their outward poverty. Many who are rich in temporals are poor in spirituals. Thus it was with the church of Laodicea. Some who are poor outwardly are inwardly rich, rich in faith and in good works, rich in privileges, rich in bonds and deeds of gift, rich in hope, rich in reversion. Spiritual riches are usually the reward of great diligence; the diligent hand makes rich. Where there is spiritual plenty, outward poverty may be better borne; and when God's people are impoverished in temporals, for the sake of Christ and a good conscience, he makes all up to them in spiritual riches, which are much more satisfying and enduring.

2. Of their sufferings: I know thy tribulation and thy poverty-the persecution they underwent, even to the spoiling of their goods. Those who will be faithful to Christ must expect to go through many tribulations; but Jesus Christ takes particular notice of all their troubles. In all their afflictions, he is afflicted, and he will recompense tribulation to those who trouble them, but to

those that are troubled rest with himself.

3. He knows the wickedness and the falsehood of their enemies: I know the blasphemy of those that say they are Jews, but are not; that is, of those who pretend to be the only peculiar covenant-people of God, as the Jews boasted themselves to be, even after God had rejected them; or of those who would be setting up the Jewish rites and ceremonies, which were now not only antiquated, but abrogated; these may say that they only are the church of God in the world, when indeed they are the synagogue of Satan. Observe, (1.) As Christ has a church in the world, the spiritual Israel of God, so the devil has his synagogue. Those assemblies which are set up in opposition to the truths of the gospel, and which promote and propagate damnable errors,-those which are set up in opposition to the purity and spirituality of gospel worship, and which promote and propagate the vain inventions of men and rites and ceremonies which never entered into the thoughts of God,-these are all synagogues of Satan: he presides over them, he works in them, his interests are served by them, and he receives a horrid homage and honour from them. (2.) For the synagogues of Satan to give themselves out to be the church or Israel of God is no less than blasphemy. God is greatly dishonoured when his name is made use of to promote and patronize the interests of Satan; and he has a high resentment of this blasphemy, and will take a just revenge on those who persist in it.

4. He foreknows the future trials of his people, and forewarns them of them, and fore-arms them against them. (1.) He forewarns them of future trials: The devil shall cast some of you into prison, and you shall have tribulation, Rev 2:10. The people of God must look for a series and succession of troubles in this world, and their troubles usually rise higher. They had been impoverished by their tribulations before; now they must be imprisoned. Observe, It is the devil that stirs up his instruments, wicked men, to persecute the people of God; tyrants and persecutors are the devil's tools, though they gratify their own sinful malignity, and know not that they are actuated by a diabolical malice. (2.) Christ fore-arms them against these approaching troubles, [1.] By his counsel: Fear none of these things. This is not only a word of command, but of efficacy, no, only forbidding slavish fear, but subduing it and furnishing the soul with strength and courage. [2.] By showing them how their sufferings would be alleviated and limited. First, They should not be universal. It would be some of them, not all, who should be cast into prison, those who were best able to bear it and might expect to be visited and comforted by the rest. Secondly, They were not to be perpetual, but for a set time, and a short time: Ten days. It should not be everlasting tribulation, the time should be shortened for the elect's sake. Thirdly, It should be to try them, not to destroy them, that their faith, and patience, and courage, might be proved and improved, and be found to honour and glory. [3.] By proposing and promising a glorious reward to their fidelity: Be thou faithful to death, and I will give thee a crown of life. Observe, First, The sureness of the reward: I will give thee. He has said it that is able to do it; and he has undertaken that he will do it. They shall have the reward from his own hand, and none of their enemies shall be able to wrest it out of his hand, or to pull it from their heads. Secondly, The suitableness of it. 1. A crown, to reward their poverty, their fidelity, and their conflict. 2. A crown of life, to reward those who are faithful even unto death, who are faithful till they die, and who part with life itself in fidelity to Christ. The life so worn out in his service, or laid down in his cause, shall be rewarded with another and a much better life that shall be eternal.

III. The conclusion of this message, and that, as before, 1. With a call to universal attention, that all men, all the world, should hear what passes between Christ and his churches-how he commends them, how he comforts them, how he reproves their failures, how he rewards their fidelity. It concerns all the inhabitants of the world to observe God's dealings with his own people; all the world may learn instruction and wisdom thereby. 2. With a gracious promise to the conquering Christian: He that overcometh shall not be hurt of the second death, Rev 2:11. Observe, (1.) There is not only a first, but a second death, a death after the body is dead. (2.) This second death is unspeakably worse than the first death, both in the dying pangs and agonies of it (which are the agonies of the soul, without any mixture of support) and in the duration; it is eternal death, dying the death, to die and to be always dying. This is hurtful indeed, fatally hurtful, to all who fall under it. (3.) From this hurtful, this destructive death, Christ will save all his faithful servants; the second death shall have no power over those who are partakers of the first resurrection: the first death shall not hurt them, and the second death shall have no power over them.

Revelation 2:12

Here also we are to consider,

I. The inscription of this message. 1. To whom it was sent: To the angel of the church of Pergamos. Whether this was a city raised up out of the ruins of old Troy, a Troy nouveau (as our London was once called), or some other city of the same name, is neither certain nor material; it was a place where Christ had called and constituted a gospel church, by the preaching of the gospel and the grace of his Spirit making the word effectual. 2. Who it was that sent this message to Pergamos: the same Jesus who here describes himself as one that hath the sharp sword with two edges (Rev 1:16), out of whose mouth went a sharp two-edged sword. Some have observed that, in the several titles of Christ which are prefixed to the several epistles, there is something suited to the state of those churches; as in that to Ephesus, what could be more proper to awaken and recover a drowsy and declining church than to hear Christ speaking as one that held the stars in his hand, and walked in the midst of the golden candlesticks? etc. The church of Pergamos was infested with men of corrupt minds, who did what they could to corrupt both the faith and manners of the church; and Christ, being resolved to fight against them by the sword of his word, takes the title of him that hath the sharp sword with two edges. (1.) The word of God is a sword; it is a weapon both offensive and defensive, it is, in the hand of God, able to slay both sin and sinners. (2.) It is a sharp sword. No heart is so hard but it is able to cut it; it can divide asunder between the soul and the spirit, that is, between the soul and those sinful habits that by custom have become another soul, or seem to be essential to it. (3.) It is a sword with two edges; it turns and cuts every way. There is the edge of the law against the transgressors of that dispensation, and the edge of the gospel against the despisers of that dispensation; there is an edge to make a wound, and an edge to open a festered wound in order to its healing. There is no escaping the edge of this sword: if you turn aside to the right hand, it has an edge on that side; if on the left hand, you fall upon the edge of the sword on that side; it turns every way.

II. From the inscription we proceed to the contents of the epistle, in which the method is much the same as is observed in the rest. Here,

1. Christ takes notice of the trials and difficulties this church encountered with: I know thy

works, and where thou dwellest, etc., Rev 2:13. The works of God's servants are best known when the circumstances under which they did those works are duly considered. Now that which added very much lustre to the good works of this church was the circumstance of the place where this church was planted, a place where Satan's seat was. As our great Lord takes notice of all the advantages and opportunities we have for duty in the places where we dwell, so he takes notice of all the temptations and discouragements we meet with from the places where we dwell, and makes gracious allowances for them. This people dwelt where Satan's seat was, where he kept his court. His circuit is throughout the world, his seat is in some places that are infamous for wickedness, error, and cruelty. Some think that the Roman governor in this city was a most violent enemy to the Christians; and the seat of persecution is Satan's seat.

2. He commends their stedfastness: Thou holdest fast my name, and hast not denied my faith. These two expressions are much the same in sense; the former may, however, signify the effect and the latter the cause or means. (1.) "Thou holdest fast my name; thou art not ashamed of thy relation to me, but accountest it thine honour that my name is named on thee, that, as the wife bears the name of the husband, so thou art called by my name; this thou holdest fast, as thine honour and privilege." (2.) "That which has made thee thus faithful is the grace of faith: thou hast not denied the great doctrines of the gospel, nor departed from the Christian faith, and by that means thou hast been kept faithful." Our faith will have a great influence upon our faithfulness. Men who deny the faith of Christ may boast very much of their sincerity, and faithfulness to God and conscience; but it has been seldom known that those who let go the true faith retained their fidelity; usually on that rock on which men make shipwreck of their faith they make shipwreck of a good conscience too. And here our blessed Lord aggrandizes the fidelity of this church from the circumstance of the times, as well as of the place where they lived: they had been stedfast even in those days wherein Antipas his faithful martyr was slain among them. Who this person was, and whether there be anything mysterious in his name, we have no certain account. He was a faithful disciple of Christ, he suffered martyrdom for it, and sealed his faith and fidelity with his blood in the place where Satan dwelt; and though the rest of the believers there knew this, and saw it, yet they were not discouraged nor drawn away from their stedfastness: this is mentioned as an addition to their honour.

3. He reproves them for their sinful failures (Rev 2:14): But I have a few things against thee, because thou hast there those that hold the doctrine of Balaam, etc., and those that hold the doctrine of the Nicolaitans, which thing I hate. There were some who taught that it was lawful to eat things sacrificed to idols, and that simple fornication was no sin; they, by an impure worship, drew men into impure practices, as Balaam did the Israelites. Observe, (1.) The filthiness of the spirit and the filthiness of the flesh often go together. Corrupt doctrines and a corrupt worship often lead to a corrupt conversation. (2.) It is very lawful to fix the name of the leaders of any heresy upon those who follow them. It is the shortest way of telling whom we mean. (3.) To continue in communion with persons of corrupt principles and practices is displeasing to God, draws a guilt and blemish upon the whole society: they become partakers of other men's sins. Though the church, as such, has no power to punish the persons of men, either for heresy or immorality, with corporal penalties, yet it has power to exclude them from its communion; and, if it do not so, Christ, the head and lawgiver of the church, will be displeased with it.

4. He calls them to repentance: Repent, or else I will come unto thee quickly, etc., Rev 2:16.

Observe here, (1.) Repentance is the duty of saints as well as sinners; it is a gospel duty. (2.) It is the duty of churches and communities as well as particular persons; those who sin together should repent together. (3.) It is the duty of Christian societies to repent of other men's sins, as far as they have been accessory to them, though but so much as by connivance. (4.) When God comes to punish the corrupt members of a church, he rebukes that church itself for allowing such to continue in its communion, and some drops of the storm fall upon the whole society. (5.) No sword cuts so deep, nor inflicts so mortal a wound, as the sword of Christ's mouth. Let but the threatenings of the word be set home upon the conscience of a sinner, and he will soon be a terror to himself; let these threatenings be executed, and the sinner is utterly cut off. The word of God will take hold of sinners, sooner or later, either for their conviction or their confusion.

III. We have the conclusion of this epistle, where, after the usual demand of universal attention, there is the promise of great favour to those that overcome. They shall eat of the hidden manna, and have the new name, and the white stone, which no man knoweth, saving he that receiveth it, Rev 2:17. 1. The hidden manna, the influences and comforts of the Spirit of Christ in communion with him, coming down from heaven into the soul, from time to time, for its support, to let it taste something how saints and angels live in heaven. This is hidden from the rest of the world-a stranger intermeddles not with this joy; and it is laid up in Christ, the ark of the covenant, in the holy of holies. 2. The white stone, with a new name engraven upon it. This white stone is absolution from the guilt of sin, alluding to the ancient custom of giving a white stone to those acquitted on trial and a black stone to those condemned. The new name is the name of adoption: adopted persons took the name of the family into which they were adopted. None can read the evidence of a man's adoption but himself; he cannot always read it, but if he persevere he shall have both the evidence of sonship and the inheritance.

Revelation 2:18

The form of each epistle is very much the same; and in this, as the rest, we have to consider the inscription, contents, and conclusion.

I. The inscription, telling us, 1. To whom it is directed: To the angel of the church of Thyatira, a city of the proconsular Asia, bordering upon Mysia on the north and Lydia on the south, a town of trade, whence came the woman named Lydia, a seller of purple, who, being at Philippi in Macedonia, probably about the business of her calling, heard Paul preach there, and God opened her heart, that she attended to the things that were spoken, and believed, and was baptized, and entertained Paul and Silas there. Whether it was by her means that the gospel was brought into her own city, Thyatira, is not certain; but that it was there, and successful to the forming of a gospel church, this epistle assures us. 2. By whom it was sent: by the Son of God, who is here described as having eyes like a flame of fire, and feet like as fine brass. His general title is here, the Son of God, that is, the eternal and only-begotten Son of God, which denotes that he has the same nature with the Father, but with a distinct and subordinate manner of subsistence. The description we have here of him is in two characters:-(1.) That his eyes are like a flame of fire, signifying his piercing, penetrating, perfect knowledge, a thorough insight into all persons and all things, one who searches the hearts and tries the reins of the children of men (Rev 2:23), and will make all the churches to know he does so. (2.) That his feet are like fine brass, that the outgoings of his providence are steady, awful, and all pure and holy. As he judges with perfect wisdom, so he acts with perfect strength and steadiness.

II. The contents or subject-matter of this epistle, which, as the rest, includes,

1. The honourable character and commendation Christ gives of this church, ministry, and people; and this given by one who was no stranger to them, but well acquainted with them and with the principles from which they acted. Now in this church Christ makes honourable mention, (1.) Of their charity, either more general, a disposition to do good to all men, or more special, to the household of faith: there is no religion where there is no charity. (2.) Their service, their ministration; this respects chiefly the officers of the church, who had laboured in the word and doctrine. (3.) Their faith, which was the grace that actuated all the rest, both their charity and their service. (4.) Their patience; for those that are most charitable to others, most diligent in their places, and most faithful, must yet expect to meet with that which will exercise their patience. (5.) Their growing fruitfulness: their last works were better than the first. This is an excellent character; when others had left their first love, and lost their first zeal, these were growing wiser and better. It should be the ambition and earnest desire of all Christians that their last works may be their best works, that they may be better and better every day, and best at last.

2. A faithful reproof for what was amiss. This is not so directly charged upon the church itself as upon some wicked seducers who were among them; the church's fault was that she connived too much at them.

(1.) These wicked seducers were compared to Jezebel, and called by her name. Jezebel was a persecutor of the prophets of the Lord, and a great patroness of idolaters and false prophets. The sin of these seducers was that they attempted to draw the servants of God into fornication, and to offer sacrifices to idols; they called themselves prophets, and so would claim a superior authority and regard to the ministers of the church. Two things aggravated the sin of these seducers, who, being one in their spirit and design, are spoken of as one person:-[1.] They made use of the name of God to oppose the truth of his doctrine and worship; this very much aggravated their sin. [2.] They abused the patience of God to harden themselves in their wickedness. God gave them space for repentance, but they repented not. Observe, First, Repentance is necessary to prevent a sinner's ruin. Secondly, Repentance requires time, a course of time, and time convenient; it is a great work, and a work of time. Thirdly, Where God gives space for repentance, he expects fruits meet for repentance. Fourthly, Where the space for repentance is lost, the sinner perishes with a double destruction.

(2.) Now why should the wickedness of this Jezebel be charged upon the church of Thyatira? Because that church suffered her to seduce the people of that city. But how could the church help it? They had not, as a church, civil power to banish or imprison her; but they had ministerial power to censure and to excommunicate her: and it is probable that neglecting to use the power they had made them sharers in her sin.

3. The punishment of this seducer, this Jezebel, Rev 2:22, Rev 2:23, in which is couched a prediction of the fall of Babylon. (1.) I will cast her into a bed, into a bed of pain, not of pleasure, into a bed of flames; and those who have sinned with her shall suffer with her; but this may yet be prevented by their repentance. (2.) I will kill her children with death; that is, the second death,

which does the work effectually, and leaves no hope of future life, no resurrection for those that are killed by the second death, but only to shame and everlasting contempt.

4. The design of Christ in the destruction of these wicked seducers, and this was the instruction of others, especially of his churches: All the churches shall know that I am he that searcheth the reins and the hearts; and I will give to every one of you according to your works. God is known by the judgments that he executes; and, by this revenge taken upon seducers, he would make known, (1.) His infallible knowledge of the hearts of men, of their principles, designs, frame, and temper, their formality, their indifference, their secret inclinations to symbolize with idolaters. (2.) His impartial justice, in giving every one according to his work, that the name of Christians should be no protection, their churches should be no sanctuaries for sin and sinners.

5. The encouragement given to those who keep themselves pure and undefiled: But to you I say, and unto the rest, etc., Rev 2:24. Observe, (1.) What these seducers called their doctrines-depths, profound mysteries, amusing the people, and endeavouring to persuade them that they had a deeper insight into religion than their own ministers had attained to. (2.) What Christ called them-depths of Satan, Satanical delusions and devices, diabolical mysteries; for there is a mystery of iniquity, as well and the great mystery of godliness. It is a dangerous thing to despise the mystery of God, and it is as dangerous to receive the mysteries of Satan. (3.) How tender Christ is of his faithful servants: "I will lay upon you no other burden; but that which you have already hold fast till I come,Rev 2:24, Rev 2:25. I will not overburden your faith with any new mysteries, nor your consciences with any new laws. I only require your attention to what you have received. Hold that fast till I come, and I desire no more." Christ is coming to put an end to all the temptations of his people; and, if they hold fast faith and a good conscience till he come, all the difficulty and danger will be over.

III. We now come to the conclusion of this message, Rev 2:26-29. Here we have, 1. The promise of an ample reward to the persevering victorious believer, in two parts:-(1.) Very great power and dominion over the rest of the world: Power over the nations, which may refer either to the time when the empire should turn Christian, and the world be under the government of the Christian emperor, as in Constantine's time; or to the other world, when believers shall sit down with Christ on his throne of judgment, and join with him in trying, and condemning, and consigning over to punishment the enemies of Christ and the church. The upright shall have dominion in the morning. (2.) Knowledge and wisdom, suitable to such power and dominion: I will give him the morning-star. Christ is the morning-star. He brings day with him into the soul, the light of grace and of glory; and he will give his people that perfection of light and wisdom which is requisite to the state of dignity and dominion that they shall have in the morning of the resurrection. 2. This epistle ends with the usual demand of attention: He that hath an ear let him hear what the Spirit saith unto the churches. In the foregoing epistles, this demand of attention comes before the concluding promise; but in this, and all that follow, it comes after, and tells us that we should all attend to the promises as well as to the precepts that Christ delivers to the churches.

Revelation Chapter 3

Revelation

Here we have three more of the epistles of Christ to the churches: I. To Sardis (Rev 3:1-6). II. To Philadelphia (Rev 3:7-13). III. To Laodicea (Rev 3:14 to the end).

Revelation 3:1

Here is, I. The preface, showing, 1. To whom this letter is directed: To the angel of the church of Sardis, an ancient city of Lydia, on the banks of the mountain Tmolus, said to have been the chief city of Asia the Less, and the first city in that part of the world that was converted by the preaching of John; and, some say, the first that revolted from Christianity, and one of the first that was laid in its ruins, in which it still lies, without any church or ministry. 2. By whom this message was sent-the Lord Jesus, who here assumes the character of him that hath the seven spirits of God, and the seven stars, taken out of Rev 1:4, where the seven spirits are said to be before the throne. (1.) He hath the seven spirits, that is, the Holy Spirit with his various powers, graces, and operations; for he is personally one, though efficaciously various, and may be said here to be seven, which is the number of the churches, and of the angels of the churches, to show that to every minister, and to every church, there is a dispensation and measure of the Spirit given for them to profit withal-a stock of spiritual influence for that minister and church to improve, both for enlargement and continuance, which measure of the Spirit is not ordinarily withdrawn from them, till they forfeit it by misimprovement. Churches have their spiritual stock and fund, as well as particular believers; and, this epistle being sent to a languishing ministry and church, they are very fitly put in mind that Christ has the seven spirits, the Spirit without measure and in perfection, to whom they may apply themselves for the reviving of his work among them. (2.) He hath the seven stars, the angels of the churches; they are disposed of by him, and accountable to him, which should make them faithful and zealous. He has ministers to employ, and spiritual influences to communicate to his ministers for the good of his church. The Holy Spirit usually works by the ministry, and the ministry will be of no efficacy without the Spirit; the same divine hand holds them both.

II. The body of this epistle. There is this observable in it, that whereas in the other epistles Christ begins with commending what is good in the churches, and then proceeds to tell them what is amiss, in this (and in the epistle to Laodicea) he begins,

1. With a reproof, and a very severe one: I know thy works, that thou hast a name that thou livest, and art dead. Hypocrisy, and a lamentable decay in religion, are the sins charged upon this church, by one who knew her well, and all her works. (1.) This church had gained a great reputation; it had a name, and a very honourable one, for a flourishing church, a name for vital lively religion, for purity of doctrine, unity among themselves, uniformity in worship, decency, and order. We read not of any unhappy divisions among themselves. Every thing appeared well, as to what falls under the observation of men. (2.) This church was not really what it was reputed to be. They had a name to live, but they were dead; there was a form of godliness, but not the

power, a name to live, but not a principle of life. If there was not a total privation of life, yet there was a great deadness in their souls and in their services, a great deadness in the spirits of their ministers, and a great deadness in their ministrations, in their praying, in their preaching, in their converse, and a great deadness in the people in hearing, in prayer, and in conversation; what little life was yet left among them was, in a manner, expiring, ready to die.

2. Our Lord proceeds to give this degenerate church the best advice: Be watchful, and strengthen the things, etc., Rev 3:2. (1.) He advises them to be upon their watch. The cause of their sinful deadness and declension was that they had let down their watch. Whenever we are off our watch, we lose ground, and therefore must return to our watchfulness against sin, and Satan, and whatever is destructive to the life and power of godliness. (2.) To strengthen the things that remain, and that are ready to die. Some understand this of persons; there were some few who had retained their integrity, but they were in danger of declining with the rest. It is a difficult thing to keep up to the life and power of godliness ourselves, when we see a universal deadness and declension prevailing round about us. Or it may be understood of practices, as it follows: I have not found thy works perfect before God, not filled up; there is something wanting in them; there is the shell, but not the kernel; there is the carcase, but not the soul-the shadow, but not the substance. The inward thing is wanting, thy works are hollow and empty; prayers are not filled up with holy desires, alms-deeds not filled up with true charity, sabbaths not filled up with suitable devotion of soul to God; there are not inward affections suitable to outward acts and expressions. Now when the spirit is wanting the form cannot long subsist. (3.) To recollect themselves, and remember how they have received and heard (Rev 3:3); not only to remember what they had received and heard, what messages they had received from God, what tokens of his mercy and favour towards them, what sermons they had heard, but how they had received and heard, what impressions the mercies of God had made upon their souls at first, what affections they felt working under their word and ordinances, the love of their espousals, the kindness of their youth, how welcome the gospel and the grace of God were to them when they first received them. Where is the blessedness they then spoke of? (4.) To hold fast what they had received, that they might not lose all, and repent sincerely that they had lost so much of the life of religion, and had run the risk of losing all.

3. Christ enforces his counsel with a dreadful threatening in case it should be despised: I will come unto thee as a thief, and thou shalt not know the hour, Rev 3:3. Observe, (1.) When Christ leaves a people as to his gracious presence, he comes to them in judgment; and his judicial presence will be very dreadful to those who have sinned away his gracious presence. (2.) His judicial approach to a dead declining people will be surprising; their deadness will keep them in security, and, as it procures an angry visit from Christ to them, it will prevent their discerning it and preparing for it. (3.) Such a visit from Christ will be to their loss; he will come as a thief, to strip them of their remaining enjoyments and mercies, not by fraud, but in justice and righteousness, taking the forfeiture they have made of all to him.

4. Our blessed Lord does not leave this sinful people without some comfort and encouragement: In the midst of judgment he remembers mercy (Rev 3:4), and here (1.) He makes honourable mention of the faithful remnant in Sardis, though but small: Thou hast a few names in Sardis which have not defiled their garments; they had not given into the prevailing corruptions and pollution of the day and place in which they lived. God takes notice of the smallest number of

those who abide with him; and the fewer they are the more precious in his sight. (2.) He makes a very gracious promise to them: They shall walk with me in white, for they are worthy-in the stola, the white robes of justification, and adoption, and comfort, or in the white robes of honour and glory in the other world. They shall walk with Christ in the pleasant walks of the heavenly paradise; and what delightful converse will there be between Christ and them when they thus walk together! This is an honour proper and suitable to their integrity, which their fidelity has prepared them for, and which it is no way unbecoming Christ to confer upon them, though it is not a legal but a gospel worthiness that is ascribed to them, not merit but meetness. Those who walk with Christ in the clean garments of real practical holiness here, and keep themselves unspotted from the world, shall walk with Christ in the white robes of honour and glory in the other world: this is a suitable reward.

III. We now come to the conclusion of this epistle, in which, as before, we have,

1. A great reward promised to the conquering Christian (Rev 3:5), and it is very much the same with what has been already mentioned: He that overcometh shall be clothed in white raiment. The purity of grace shall be rewarded with the perfect purity of glory. Holiness, when perfected, shall be its own reward; glory is the perfection of grace, differing not in kind, but in degree. Now to this is added another promise very suitable to the case: I will not blot his name out of the book of life, but will confess his name before my Father, and before his angels. Observe, (1.) Christ has his book of life, a register and roll of all who shall inherit eternal life. [1.] The book of eternal election. [2.] The book of remembrance of all those who have lived to God, and have kept up the life and power of godliness in evil times. (2.) Christ will not blot the names of his chosen and faithful ones out of this book of life; men may be enrolled in the registers of the church, as baptized, as making a profession, as having a name to live, and that name may come to be blotted out of the roll, when it appears that it was but a name, a name to live, without spiritual life; such often lose the very name before they die, they are left of God to blot out their own names by their gross and open wickedness. But the names of those that overcome shall never be blotted out. (3.) Christ will produce this book of life, and confess the names of the faithful who stand there, before God, and all the angels; he will do this as their Judge, when the books shall be opened; he will do this as their captain and head, leading them with him triumphantly to heaven, presenting them to the Father: Behold me, and the children that thou hast given me. How great will this honour and reward be!

2. The demand of universal attention finishes the message. Every word from God deserves attention from men; that which may seem more particularly directed to one body of men has something in it instructive to all.

Revelation 3:7

We have now come to the sixth letter, sent to one of the Asian churches, where observe,

I. The inscription, showing,

1. For whom it was more immediately designed: The angel of the church of Philadelphia; this also was a city in Asia Minor, seated upon the borders of Mysia and Lydia, and had its name

xxiii

from that brotherly love for which it was eminent. We can hardly suppose that this name was given to it after it received the Christian religion, and that it was so called from that Christian affection that all believers have, and should have, one for another, as the children of one Father and the brethren of Christ; but rather that it was its ancient name, on account of the love and kindness which the citizens had and showed to each other as a civil fraternity. This was an excellent spirit, and, when sanctified by the grace of the gospel, would render them an excellent church, as indeed they were, for here is no one fault found with this church, and yet, doubtless, there were faults in it of common infirmity; but love covers such faults.

2. By whom this letter was signed; even by the same Jesus who is alone the universal head of all the churches; and here observe by what title he chooses to represent himself to this church: He that is holy, he that is true, he that hath the key of David, etc. You have his personal character: He that is holy and he that is true, holy in his nature, and therefore he cannot but be true to his word, for he hath spoken in his holiness; and you have also his political character: He hath the key of David, he openeth, and no man shutteth; he hath the key of the house of David, the key of government and authority in and over the church. Observe, (1.) The acts of his government. [1.] He opens. He opens a door of opportunity to his churches; he opens a door of utterance to his ministers; he opens a door of entrance, opens the heart; he opens a door of admission into the visible church, laying down the terms of communion; and he opens the door of admission into the church triumphant, according to the terms of salvation fixed by him. [2.] He shuts the door. When he pleases, he shuts the door of opportunity and the door of utterance, and leaves obstinate sinners shut up in the hardness of their hearts; he shuts the door of church-fellowship against unbelievers and profane persons; and he shuts the door of heaven against the foolish virgins who have slept away their day of grace, and against the workers of iniquity, how vain and confident soever they may be. (2.) The way and manner in which he performs these acts, and that is absolute sovereignty, independent upon the will of men, and irresistible by the power of men: He openeth, and no man shutteth; he shutteth, and no man openeth; he works to will and to do, and, when he works, none can hinder. These were proper characters for him, when speaking to a church that had endeavoured to be conformed to Christ in holiness and truth, and that had enjoyed a wide door of liberty and opportunity under his care and government.

II. The subject-matter of this epistle, where,

1. Christ puts them in mind of what he had done for them: I have set before thee an open door, and no man can shut it, Rev 3:8. I have set it open, and kept it open, though there be many adversaries. Learn here, (1.) Christ is to be acknowledged as the author of all the liberty and opportunity his churches enjoy. (2.) He takes notice and keeps account, how long he has preserved their spiritual liberties and privileges for them. (3.) Wicked men envy the people of God their door of liberty, and would be glad to shut it against them. (4.) If we do not provoke Christ to shut this door against us, men cannot do it.

2. This church is commended: Thou hast a little strength, and hast kept my word, and hast not denied my name, Rev 3:8. In this there seems to be couched a gentle reproof: "Thou hast a little strength, a little grace, which, though it be not proportionate to the wide door of opportunity which I have opened to thee, yet is true grace, and has kept thee faithful." True grace, though weak, has the divine approbation; but, though Christ accepts a little strength, yet believers should

not rest satisfied in a little, but should strive to grow in grace, to be strong in faith, giving glory to God. True grace, though weak, will do more than the greatest gifts or highest degrees of common grace, for it will enable the Christian to keep the word of Christ, and not to deny his name. Obedience, fidelity, and a free confession of the name of Christ, are the fruits of true grace, and are pleasing to Christ as such.

3. Here is a promise of the great favour God would bestow on this church, Rev 3:9, Rev 3:10. This favour consists in two things:-

(1.) Christ would make this church's enemies subject to her. [1.] Those enemies are described to be such as said they were Jews, but lied in saying so-pretended to be the only and peculiar people of God, but were really the synagogue of Satan. Assemblies that worship God in spirit and in truth are the Israel of God; assemblies that either worship false gods, or the true God in a false manner, are the synagogues of Satan: though they may profess to be the only people of God, their profession is a lie. [2.] Their subjection to the church is described: They shall worship at thy feet; not pay a religious and divine honour to the church itself, nor to the ministry of it, but shall be convinced that they have been in the wrong, that this church is in the right and is beloved of Christ, and they shall desire to be taken into communion with her and that they may worship the same God after the same manner. How shall this great change be wrought? By the power of God upon the hearts of his enemies, and by signal discoveries of his peculiar favour to his church: They shall know that I have loved thee. Observe, First, The greatest honour and happiness any church can enjoy consist in the peculiar love and favour of Christ. Secondly, Christ can discover this his favour to his people in such a manner that their very enemies shall see it, and be forced to acknowledge it. Thirdly, This will, by the grace of Christ, soften the hearts of their enemies, and make them desirous to be admitted into communion with them.

(2.) Another instance of favour that Christ promises to this church is persevering grace in the most trying times (Rev 3:10), and this as the reward of their past fidelity. To him that hath shall be given. Here observe, [1.] The gospel of Christ is the word of his patience. It is the fruit of the patience of God to a sinful world; it sets before men the exemplary patience of Christ in all his sufferings for men; it calls those that receive it to the exercise of patience in conformity to Christ. [2.] This gospel should be carefully kept by all that enjoy it; they must keep up to the faith, and practice, and worship prescribed in the gospel. [3.] After a day of patience we must expect an hour of temptation; a day of gospel peace and liberty is a day of God's patience, and it is seldom so well improved as it should be and therefore it is often followed by an hour of trial and temptation. [4.] Sometimes the trial is more general and universal; it comes upon all the world, and, when it is so general, it is usually the shorter. [5.] Those who keep the gospel in a time of peace shall be kept by Christ in an hour of temptation. By keeping the gospel they are prepared for the trial; and the same divine grace that has made them fruitful in times of peace will make them faithful in times of persecution.

4. Christ calls the church to that duty which he before promised he would enable her to do, and that is, to persevere, to hold fast that which she had. (1.) The duty itself: "Hold fast that which thou hast, that faith, that truth, that strength of grace, that zeal, that love to the brethren; thou hast been possessed of this excellent treasure, hold it fast." (2.) The motives, taken from the speedy appearance of Christ: "Behold, I come quickly. See, I am just a coming to relieve them under the

trial, to reward their fidelity, and to punish those who fall away; they shall lose that crown which they once seemed to have a right to, which they hoped for, and pleased themselves with the thoughts of. The persevering Christian shall win the prize from backsliding professors, who once stood fair for it."

III. The conclusion of this epistle, Rev 3:12, Rev 3:13. Here,

1. After his usual manner, our Saviour promises a glorious reward to the victorious believer, in two things:-(1.) He shall be a monumental pillar in the temple of God; not a pillar to support the temple (heaven needs no such props), but a monument of the free and powerful grace of God, a monument that shall never be defaced nor removed, as many stately pillars erected in honour to the Roman emperors and generals have been. (2.) On this monumental pillar there shall be an honourable inscription, as in those cases is usual. [1.] The name of God, in whose cause he engaged, whom he served, and for whom he suffered in this warfare; and the name of the city of God, the church of God, the new Jerusalem, which came down from heaven. On this pillar shall be recorded all the services the believer did to the church of God, how he asserted her rights, enlarged her borders, maintained her purity and honour; this will be a greater name than Asiaticus, or Africanus; a soldier under God in the wars of the church. And then another part of the inscription is, [2.] The new name of Christ, the Mediator, the Redeemer, the captain of our salvation; by this it will appear under whose banner this conquering believer had enlisted, under whose conduct he acted, by whose example he was encouraged, and under whose influence he fought the good fight, and came off victorious.

2. The epistle is closed up with the demand of attention: He that hath an ear, let him hear what the Spirit saith unto the churches, how Christ loves and values his faithful people, how he commends, and how he will crown their fidelity.

Revelation 3:14

We now come to the last and worst of all the seven Asian churches, the reverse of the church of Philadelphia; for, as there was nothing reproved in that, here is nothing commended in this, and yet this was one of the seven golden candlesticks, for a corrupt church may still be a church. Here we have, as before,

I. The inscription, to whom, and from whom. 1. To whom: To the angel of the church of Laodicea. This was a once famous city near the river Lycus, had a wall of vast compass, and three marble theatres, and, like Rome, was built on seven hills. It seems, the apostle Paul was very instrumental in planting the gospel in this city, from which he wrote a letter, as he mentions in the epistle to the Colossians, the last chapter, in which he sends salutations to them, Laodicea not being above twenty miles distant from Colosse. In this city was held a council in the fourth century, but it has been long since demolished, and lies in its ruins to this day, an awful monument of the wrath of the Lamb. 2. From whom this message was sent. Here our Lord Jesus styles himself the Amen, the faithful and true witness, the beginning of the creation of God. (1.) The Amen, one that is steady and unchangeable in all his purposes and promises, which are all yea, and all amen. (2.) The faithful and true witness, whose testimony of God to men ought to be received and fully believed, and whose testimony of men to God will be fully believed and regarded, and will be a swift but true witness against all indifferent lukewarm professors. (3.) The beginning of the creation of God, either of the first creation, and so he is the beginning, that is, the first cause, the Creator, and the Governor of it; or of the second creation, the church; and so he is the head of that body, the first-born from the dead, as it is in Rev 1:5, whence these titles are taken. Christ, having raised up himself by his own divine power, as the head of a new world, raises up dead souls to be a living temple and church to himself.

II. The subject-matter, in which observe,

1. The heavy charge drawn up against this church, ministers and people, by one who knew them better than they knew themselves: Thou art neither cold nor hot, but worse than either; I would thou wert cold or hot, Rev 3:15. Lukewarmness or indifference in religion is the worst temper in the world. If religion is a real thing, it is the most excellent thing, and therefore we should be in good earnest in it; if it is not a real thing, it is the vilest imposture, and we should be earnest against it. If religion is worth any thing, it is worth every thing; an indifference here is inexcusable: Why halt you between two opinions? If God be God, follow him; if Baal (be God), follow him. Here is no room for neutrality. An open enemy shall have a fairer quarter than a perfidious neuter; and there is more hope of a heathen than of such. Christ expects that men should declare themselves in earnest either for him or against him.

2. A severe punishment threatened: I will spue thee out of my mouth. As lukewarm water turns the stomach, and provokes to a vomit, lukewarm professors turn the heart of Christ against them. He is sick of them, and cannot long bear them. They may call their lukewarmness charity, meekness, moderation, and a largeness of soul; it is nauseous to Christ, and makes those so that allow themselves in it. They shall be rejected, and finally rejected; for far be it from the holy Jesus to return to that which has been thus rejected.

3. We have one cause of this indifference and inconsistency in religion assigned, and that is self-conceitedness or self-delusion. They thought they were very well already, and therefore they were very indifferent whether they grew better or no: Because thou sayest, I am rich, and increased with goods, etc., Rev 3:17. Here observe, What a difference there was between the thoughts they had of themselves and the thoughts that Christ had of them. (1.) The high thoughts they had of themselves: Thou sayest, I am rich, and increased with goods, and have need of nothing, rich, and growing richer, and increased to such a degree as to be above all want or possibility of wanting. Perhaps they were well provided for as to their bodies, and this made them overlook the necessities of their souls. Or they thought themselves well furnished in their souls: they had learning, and they took it for religion; they had gifts, and they took them for grace; they had wit, and they took it for true wisdom; they had ordinances, and they took up with them instead of the God of ordinances. How careful should we be not to put the cheat upon our own souls! Doubtless there are many in hell that once thought themselves to be in the way to heaven. Let us daily beg of God that we may not be left to flatter and deceive ourselves in the concerns of our souls. (2.) The mean thoughts that Christ had of them; and he was not mistaken. He knew, though they knew not, that they were wretched, and miserable, and poor, and blind, and naked. Their state was wretched in itself, and such as called for pity and compassion from others: though they were proud of themselves, they were pitied by all who knew their case. For, [1.] They were poor, really poor, when they said and thought they were rich; they had no

provision for their souls to live upon; their souls were starving in the midst of their abundance; they were vastly in debt to the justice of God, and had nothing to pay off the least part of the debt. [2.] They were blind; they could not see their state, nor their way, nor their danger; they could not see into themselves; they could not look before them; they were blind, and yet they thought they saw; the very light that was in them was darkness, and then how great must that darkness be! They could not see Christ, though evidently set forth, and crucified, before their eyes. They could not see God by faith, though always present in them. They could not see death, though it was just before them. They could not look into eternity, though they stood upon the very brink of it continually. [3.] They were naked, without clothing and without house and harbour for their souls. They were without clothing, had neither the garment of justification nor that of sanctification. Their nakedness both of guilt and pollution had no covering. They lay always exposed to sin and shame. Their righteousnesses were but filthy rags; they were rags, and would not cover them, filthy rags, and would defile them. And they were naked, without house or harbour, for they were without God, and he has been the dwelling-place of his people in all ages; in him alone the soul of man can find rest, and safety, and all suitable accommodations. The riches of the body will not enrich the soul; the sight of the body will not enlighten the soul; the most convenient house for the body will not afford rest nor safety to the soul. The soul is a different thing from the body, and must have accommodation suitable to its nature, or else in the midst of bodily prosperity it will be wretched and miserable.

4. We have good counsel given by Christ to this sinful people, and that is that they drop their vain and false opinion they had of themselves, and endeavour to be that really which they would seem to be: I counsel thee to buy of me, etc.,Rev 3:18. Observe, (1.) Our Lord Jesus Christ continues to give good counsel to those who have cast his counsels behind their backs. (2.) The condition of sinners in never desperate, while they enjoy the gracious calls and counsels of Christ. (3.) Our blessed Lord, the counsellor, always gives the best advice, and that which is most suitable to the sinner's case; as here, [1.] These people were poor; Christ counsels them to buy of him gold tried in the fire, that they might be rich. He lets them know where they might have true riches and how they might have them. First, Where they might have them-from himself; he sends them not to the streams of Pactolus, nor to the mines of Potosi, but invites them to himself, the pearl of price. Secondly, And how must they have this true gold from him? They must buy it. This seems to be unsaying all again. How can those that are poor buy gold? Just as they may buy of Christ wine and milk, that is, without money and without price, Isa 55:1. Something indeed must be parted with, but it is nothing of a valuable consideration, it is only to make room for receiving true riches. "Part with sin and self-sufficiency, and come to Christ with a sense of your poverty and emptiness, that you may be filled with his hidden treasure." [2.] These people were naked; Christ tells them where they might have clothing, and such as would cover the shame of their nakedness. This they must receive from Christ; and they must only put off their filthy rags that they might put on the white raiment which he had purchased and provided for them-his own imputed righteousness for justification and the garments of holiness and sanctification. [3.] They were blind; and he counsels them to buy of him eye-salve, that they might see, to give up their own wisdom and reason, which are but blindness in the things of God, and resign themselves to his word and Spirit, and their eyes shall be opened to see their way and their end, their duty and their true interest; a new and glorious scene would then open itself to their souls; a new world furnished with the most beautiful and excellent objects, and this light would be marvellous to those who were but just now delivered from the powers of darkness.

This is the wise and good counsel Christ gives to careless souls; and, if they follow it, he will judge himself bound in honour to make it effectual.

5. Here is added great and gracious encouragement to this sinful people to take the admonition and advice well that Christ had given them, Rev 3:19, Rev 3:20. He tells them, (1.) It was given them in true and tender affection: "Whom I love, I rebuke and chasten. You may think I have given you hard words and severe reproofs; it is all out of love to your souls. I would not have thus openly rebuked and corrected your sinful lukewarmness and vain confidence, if I had not been a lover of your souls; had I hated you, I would have let you alone, to go on in sin till it had been your ruin." Sinners ought to take the rebukes of God's word and rod as tokens of his good-will to their souls, and should accordingly repent in good earnest, and turn to him that smites them; better are the frowns and wounds of a friend than the flattering smiles of an enemy. (2.) If they would comply with his admonitions, he was ready to make them good to their souls: Behold, I stand at the door and knock, etc., Rev 3:20. Here observe, [1.] Christ is graciously pleased by his word and Spirit to come to the door of the heart of sinners; he draws near to them in a way of mercy, ready to make them a kind visit. [2.] He finds this door shut against him; the heart of man is by nature shut up against Christ by ignorance, unbelief, sinful prejudices. [3.] When he finds the heart shut, he does not immediately withdraw, but he waits to be gracious, even till his head be filled with the dew. [4.] He uses all proper means to awaken sinners, and to cause them to open to him: he calls by his word, he knocks by the impulses of his Spirit upon their conscience. [5.] Those who open to him shall enjoy his presence, to their great comfort and advantage. He will sup with them; he will accept of what is good in them; he will eat his pleasant fruit; and he will bring the best part of the entertainment with him. If what he finds would make but a poor feast, what he brings will make up the deficiency: he will give fresh supplies of graces and comforts, and thereby stir up fresh actings of faith, and love, and delight; and in all this Christ and his repenting people will enjoy pleasant communion with each other. Alas! what do careless obstinate sinners lose by refusing to open the door of the heart to Christ!

III. We now come to the conclusion of this epistle; and here we have as before,

1. The promise made to the overcoming believer. It is here implied, (1.) That though this church seemed to be wholly overrun and overcome with lukewarmness and self-confidence, yet it was possible that by the reproofs and counsels of Christ they might be inspired with fresh zeal and vigour, and might come off conquerors in their spiritual warfare. (2.) That, if they did so, all former faults should be forgiven, and they should have a great reward. And what is that reward? They shall sit down with me on my throne, as I also overcame, and have sat down with my Father on his throne, Rev 3:21. Here it is intimated, [1.] That Christ himself had met with his temptations and conflicts. [2.] That he overcame them all, and was more than a conqueror. [3.] That, as the reward of his conflict and victory, he has sat down with God the Father on his throne, possessed of that glory which he had with the Father from eternity, but which he was pleased very much to conceal on earth, leaving it as it were in the hands of the Father, as a pledge that he would fulfil the work of a Saviour before he reassumed that manifestative glory; and, having done so, then pignus reposcere-he demands the pledge, to appear in his divine glory equal to the Father. [4.] That those who are conformed to Christ in his trials and victories shall be conformed to him in his glory; they shall sit down with him on his throne, on his throne of judgment at the end of the world, on his throne of glory to all eternity, shining in his beams by

virtue of their union with him and relation to him, as the mystical body of which he is the head.

2. All is closed up with the general demand of attention (Rev 3:22), putting all to whom these epistles shall come in mind that what is contained in them is not of private interpretation, not intended for the instruction, reproof, and correction of those particular churches only, but of all the churches of Christ in all ages and parts of the world: and as there will be a resemblance in all succeeding churches to these, both in their graces and sins, so they may expect that God will deal with them as he dealt with these, which are patterns to all ages what faithful, and fruitful churches may expect to receive from God, and what those who are unfaithful may expect to suffer from his hand; yea, that God's dealings with his churches may afford useful instruction to the rest of the world, to put them upon considering, If judgment begin at the house of God, what shall the end of those be that do not obey the gospel of Christ? Pe1 4:17. Thus end the messages of Christ to the Asian churches, the epistolary part of this book. We now come to the prophetical part.

Revelation Chapter 4

Revelation

In this chapter the prophetical scene opens; and, as the epistolary part opened with a vision of Christ (ch. 1), so this part is introduced with a glorious appearance of the great God, whose throne is in heaven, compassed about with the heavenly host. This discovery was made to John, and in this chapter he, I. Records the heavenly sight he saw (Rev 4:1-7). And then, II. The heavenly songs he heard (Rev 4:8 to the end).

Revelation 4:1

We have here an account of a second vision with which the apostle John was favoured: After this, that is, not only "after I had seen the vision of Christ walking in the midst of the golden candlesticks," but "after I had taken his messages from his mouth, and written and sent them to the several churches, according to his command, after this I had another vision." Those who well improve the discoveries they have had of God already are prepared thereby for more, and may expect them. Observe,

I. The preparation made for the apostle's having this vision.

1. A door was opened in heaven. Hence we learn, (1.) Whatever is transacted on earth is first designed and settled in heaven; there is the model of all the works of God; all of them are therefore before his eye, and he lets the inhabitants of heaven see as much of them as is fit for them. (2.) We can know nothing of future events but what God is pleased to discover to us; they are within the veil, till God opens the door. But, (3.) So far as God reveals his designs to us we may and ought to receive them, and not pretend to be wise above what is revealed.

2. To prepare John for the vision, a trumpet was sounded, and he was called up into heaven, to have a sight there of the things which were to be hereafter. He was called into the third heavens. (1.) There is a way opened into the holiest of all, into which the sons of God may enter by faith and holy affections now, in their spirits when they die, and in their whole persons at the last day. (2.) We must not intrude into the secret of God's presence, but stay till we are called up to it.

3. To prepare for this vision, the apostle was in the Spirit. He was in a rapture, as before (Rev 1:10), whether in the body or out of the body we cannot tell; perhaps he himself could not; however all bodily actions and sensations were for a time suspended, and his spirit was possessed with the spirit of prophecy, and wholly under a divine influence. The more we abstract ourselves from all corporeal things the more fit we are for communion with God; the body is a veil, a cloud, and clog to the mind in its transactions with God. We should as it were forget it when we go in before the Lord in duty, and be willing to drop it, that we may go up to him in heaven. This was the apparatus to the vision. Now observe,

II. The vision itself. It begins with the strange sights that the apostle saw, and they were such as these:-1. He saw a throne set in heaven, the seat of honour, and authority, and judgment. Heaven is the throne of God; there he resides in glory, and thence he gives laws to the church and to the whole world, and all earthly thrones are under the jurisdiction of this throne that is set in heaven. 2. He saw a glorious one upon the throne. This throne was not empty; there was one in it who filled it, and that was God, who is here described by those things that are most pleasant and precious in our world: His countenance was like a jasper and a sardine-stone; he is not described by any human features, so as to be represented by an image, but only by his transcendent brightness. This jasper is a transparent stone, which yet offers to the eye a variety of the most vivid colours, signifying the glorious perfections of God; the sardine-stone is red, signifying the justice of God, that essential attribute of which he never divests himself in favour of any, but gloriously exerts it in the government of the world, and especially of the church, through our Lord Jesus Christ. This attribute is displayed in pardoning as well as in punishing, in saving as well as in destroying sinners. 3. He saw a rainbow about the throne, like unto an emerald, Rev 4:3. The rainbow was the seal and token of the covenant of the providence that God made with Noah and his posterity with him, and is a fit emblem of that covenant of promise that God has made with Christ as the head of the church, and all his people in him, which covenant is as the waters of Noah unto God, an everlasting covenant, ordered in all things and sure. This rainbow looked like the emerald; the most prevailing colour was a pleasant green, to show the reviving and refreshing nature of the new covenant. 4. He saw four-and-twenty seats round about the throne, not empty, but filled with four-and-twenty elders, presbyters, representing, very probably, the whole church of God, both in the Old Testament and in the New Testament state; not the ministers of the church, but rather the representatives of the people. Their sitting denotes their honour, rest, and satisfaction; their sitting about the throne signifies their relation to God, their nearness to him, the sight and enjoyment they have of him. They are clothed in white raiment, the righteousness of the saints, both imputed and inherent; they had on their heads crowns of gold, signifying the honour and authority given them of God, and the glory they have with him. All these may in a lower sense be applied to the gospel church on earth, in its worshipping assemblies; and, in the higher sense, to the church triumphant in heaven. 5. He perceived lightnings and voices proceeding out of the throne; that is, the awful declarations that God makes to his church of his sovereign will and pleasure. Thus he gave forth the law on mount Sinai; and the gospel has not less glory and authority than the law, though it be of a more spiritual nature. 6. He saw seven lamps of fire burning before the throne, which are explained to be the seven Spirits of God (Rev 4:5), the various gifts, graces, and operations of the Spirit of God in the churches of Christ; these are all dispensed according to the will and pleasure of him who sits upon the throne. 7. He saw before the throne a sea of glass, like unto crystal. As in the temple there was a great vessel of brass filled with water, in which the priests were to wash when they went to minister before the Lord (and this was called a sea), so in the gospel church the sea or laver for purification is the blood of the Lord Jesus Christ, who cleanses from all sin, even from sanctuary-sins. In this all those must be washed that are admitted into the gracious presence of God on earth or his glorious presence in heaven. 8. He saw four animals, living creatures, between the throne and the circle of elders (as seems most probable), standing between God and the people; these seem to signify the ministers of the gospel, not only because of this their situation nearer to God, and between him and the elders or representatives of the Christian people, and because fewer in number than the people, but as they are here described, (1.) By their many eyes, denoting sagacity, vigilance, and circumspection. (2.) By their lion-like courage, their great labour and diligence (in which they resemble the ox), their prudence and discretion becoming men, and their sublime affections and speculations, by which they mount up with wings like eagles towards heaven (Rev 4:7), and these wings full of eyes within, to show that in all their meditations and ministrations they are to act with knowledge, and especially should be well acquainted with themselves and the state of their own souls, and see their own concern in the great doctrines and duties of religion, watching over their own souls as well as the souls of the people. (3.) By their continual employment, and that is, praising God, and not ceasing to do so night and day. The elders sit and are ministered unto; these stand and minister: they rest not night nor day. This now leads to the other part of the representation.

Revelation 4:8

We have considered the sights that the apostle saw in heaven: now let us observe the songs that he heard, for there is in heaven not only that to be seen which will highly please a sanctified eye, but there is that to be heard which will greatly delight a sanctified ear. This is true concerning the church of Christ here, which is a heaven upon earth, and it will be eminently so in the church made perfect in the heaven of heavens.

I. He heard the song of the four living creatures, of the ministers of the church, which refers to the prophet Isaiah's vision, Isa 6:1-13. And here, 1. They adore one God, and one only, the Lord God Almighty, unchangeable and everlasting. 2. They adore three holies in this one God, the Holy Father, the Holy Son, and the Holy Spirit; and these are one infinitely holy and eternal Being, who sits upon the throne, and lives for ever and ever. In this glory the prophet saw Christ, and spoke of him.

II. He heard the adorations of the four-and-twenty elders, that is, of the Christian people represented by them; the ministers led, and the people followed, in the praises of God, Rev 4:10, Rev 4:11. Here observe,

1. The object of their worship, the same with that which the ministers adored: Him that sat on the throne, the eternal everliving God. The true church of God has one and the same object of worship. Two different objects of worship, either co-ordinate or sub-ordinate, would confound the worship and divide the worshippers. It is unlawful to join in divine worship with those who either mistake or multiply the object. There is but one God, and he alone, as God, is worshipped by the church on earth and in heaven.

2. The acts of adoration. (1.) They fell down before him that sat on the throne; they discovered the most profound humility, reverence, and godly fear. (2.) They cast their crowns before the throne; they gave God the glory of the holiness wherewith he had crowned their souls on earth and the honour and happiness with which he crowns them in heaven. They owe all their graces and all their glories to him, and acknowledge that his crown is infinitely more glorious than theirs, and that it is their glory to be glorifying God.

3. The words of adoration: they said, Thou art worthy, O Lord, to receive glory, and honour, and power, Rev 4:11. Observe, (1.) They do not say, We give thee glory, and honour, and power; for what can any creature pretend to give unto God? But they say, thou art worthy to receive glory. (2.) In this they tacitly acknowledge that God is exalted far above all blessing and praise. He was

xxxiii

worthy to receive glory, but they were not worthy to praise, nor able to do it according to his infinite excellences.

4. We have the ground and reason of their adoration, which is threefold:-(1.) He is the Creator of all things, the first cause; and none but the Creator of all things should be adored; no made thing can be the object of religious worship. (2.) He is the preserver of all things, and his preservation is a continual creation; they are created still by the sustaining power of God. All beings but God are dependent upon the will and power of God, and no dependent being must be set up as an object of religious worship. It is the part of the best dependent beings to be worshippers, not to be worshipped. (3.) He is the final cause of all things: For thy pleasure they are and were created. It was his will and pleasure to create all things; he was not put upon it by the will of another; there is no such thing as a subordinate creator, that acts under and by the will and power of another; and, if there were, he ought not to be worshipped. As God made all things at his pleasure, so he made them for his pleasure, to deal with them as he pleases and to glorify himself by them one way or other. Though he delights not in the death of sinners, but rather that they should turn and live, yet he hath made all things for himself, Pro 16:4. Now if these be true and sufficient grounds for religious worship, as they are proper to God alone, Christ must needs be God, one with the Father and Spirit, and be worshipped as such; for we find the same causality ascribed to him. Col 1:16, Col 1:17, All things were created by him and for him, and he is before all things, and by him all things consist.

Revelation Chapter 5

In the foregoing chapter the prophetical scene was opened, in the sight and hearing of the apostle, and he had a sight of God the Creator and ruler of the world, and the great King of the church. He saw God on the throne of glory and government, surrounded with his holy ones, and receiving their adorations. Now the counsels and decrees of God are set before the apostle, as in a book, which God held in his right hand; and this book is represented, I. As sealed in the hand of God (Rev 5:1-9). II. As taken into the hand of Christ the Redeemer, to be unsealed and opened (Rev 5:6 to the end).

Revelation 5:1

Hitherto the apostle had seen only the great God, the governor of all things, now,

I. He is favoured with a sight of the model and methods of his government, as they are all written down in a book which he holds in his hand; and this we are now to consider as shut up and sealed in the hand of God. Observe, 1. The designs and methods of divine Providence towards the church and the world are stated and fixed; they are resolved upon and agreed to, as that which is written in a book. The great design is laid, every part adjusted, all determined, and every thing passed into decree and made a matter of record. The original and first draught of this book is the book of God's decrees, laid up in his own cabinet, in his eternal mind: but there is a transcript of so much as was necessary to be known in the book of the scriptures in general, in the prophetical part of the scripture especially, and in this prophecy in particular. 2. God holds this book in his right hand, to declare the authority of the book, and his readiness and resolution to execute all the contents thereof, all the counsels and purposes therein recorded. 3. This book in the hand of God is shut up and sealed; it is known to none but himself, till he allows it to be opened. Known unto God, and to him alone, are all his works, from the beginning of the world; but it is his glory to conceal the matter as he pleases. The times and seasons, and their great events, he hath kept in his own hand and power. 4. It is sealed with seven seals. This tells us with what inscrutable secrecy the counsels of God are laid, how impenetrable by the eye and intellect of the creature; and also points us to seven several parts of this book of God's counsels. Each part seems to have its particular seal, and, when opened, discovers its proper events; these seven parts are not unsealed and opened at once, but successively, one scene of Providence introducing another, and explaining it, till the whole mystery of God's counsel and conduct be finished in the world.

II. He heard a proclamation made concerning this sealed book. 1. The crier was a strong angel; not that there are any weak ones among the angels in heaven, though there are many among the angels of the churches. This angel seems to come out, not only as a crier, but as a champion, with a challenge to any or all the creatures to try the strength of their wisdom in opening the counsels of God; and, as a champion, he cried with a loud voice, that every creature might hear. 2. The cry or challenge proclaimed was, "Who is worthy to open the book, and to loose the seals thereof?

Rev 5:2. If there by any creature who thinks himself sufficient either to explain or execute the counsels of God, let him stand forth, and make the attempt." 3. None in heaven or earth could accept the challenge and undertake the task: none in heaven, none of the glorious holy angels, though before the throne of God, and the ministers of his providence; they with all their wisdom cannot dive into the decrees of God: none on earth, no man, the wisest or the best of men, none of the magicians and soothsayers, none of the prophets of God, any further than he reveals his mind to them: none under the earth, none of the fallen angels, none of the spirits of men departed, though they should return to our world, can open this book. Satan himself, with all his subtlety, cannot do it; the creatures cannot open it, nor look on it; they cannot read it. God only can do it.

III. He felt a great concern in himself about this matter: the apostle wept much; it was a great disappointment to him. By what he had seen in him who sat upon the throne, he was very desirous to see and know more of his mind and will: this desire, when not presently gratified, filled him with sorrow, and fetched many tears from his eyes. Here observe, 1. Those who have seen most of God in this world are most desirous to see more; and those who have seen his glory desire to know his will. 2. Good men may be too eager and to hasty to look into the mysteries of divine conduct. 3. Such desires, not presently answered, turn to grief and sorrow. Hope deferred makes the heart sick.

IV. The apostle was comforted and encouraged to hope this sealed book would yet be opened. Here observe, 1. Who it was that gave John the hint: One of the elders. God had revealed it to his church. If angels do not refuse to learn from the church, ministers should not disdain to do it. God can make his people to instruct and inform their teachers when he pleases. 2. Who it was that would do the thing-the Lord Jesus Christ, called the lion of the tribe of Judah, according to his human nature, alluding to Jacob's prophecy (Gen 49:10), and the root of David according to his divine nature, though a branch of David according to the flesh. He who is a middle person, God and man, and bears the office of Mediator between God and man, is fit and worthy to open and execute all the counsels of God towards men. And this he does in his mediatorial state and capacity, as the root of David and the offspring of Judah, and as the King and head of the Israel of God; and he will do it, to the consolation and joy of all his people.

Revelation 5:6

Here, I. The apostle beholds this book taken into the hands of the Lord Jesus Christ, in order to its being unsealed and opened by him. Here Christ is described, 1. By his place and station: In the midst of the throne, and of the four beasts, and of the elders. He was on the same throne with the Father; he was nearer to him than either the elders or ministers of the churches. Christ, as man and Mediator, is subordinate to God the Father, but is nearer to him than all the creatures; for in him all the fulness of the Godhead dwells bodily. The ministers stand between God and the people. Christ stands as the Mediator between God and both ministers and people. 2. The form in which he appeared. Before he is called a lion; here he appears as a lamb slain. He is a lion to conquer Satan, a lamb to satisfy the justice of God. He appears with the marks of his sufferings upon him, to show that he interceded in heaven in the virtue of his satisfaction. He appears as a lamb, having seven horns and seven eyes, perfect power to execute all the will of God and perfect wisdom to understand it all and to do it in the most effectual manner; for he hath the seven Spirits of God, he has received the Holy Spirit without measure, in all perfection of light, and life, and power, by which he is able to teach and rule all parts of the earth. 3. He is described by his act and deed: He came, and took the book out of the right hand of him that sat on the throne (Rev 5:7), not by violence, nor by fraud, but he prevailed to do it (as Rev 5:5), he prevailed by his merit and worthiness, he did it by authority and by the Father's appointment. God very willingly and justly put the book of his eternal counsels into the hand of Christ, and Christ as readily and gladly took it into his hand; for he delights to reveal and to do the will of his Father.

II. The apostle observes the universal joy and thanksgiving that filled heaven and earth upon this transaction. No sooner had Christ received this book out of the Father's hand than he received the applauses and adorations of angels and men, yea, of every creature. And, indeed, it is just matter of joy to all the world to see that God does not deal with men in a way of absolute power and strict justice, but in a way of grace and mercy through the Redeemer. He governs the world, not merely as a Creator and Lawgiver, but as our God and Saviour. All the world has reason to rejoice in this. The song of praise that was offered up to the Lamb on this occasion consists of three parts, one part sung by the church, another by the church and the angels, the third by every creature.

1. The church begins the doxology, as being more immediately concerned in it (Rev 5:8), the four living creatures, and the four-and-twenty elders, the Christian people, under their minister, lead up the chorus. Here observe, (1.) The object of their worship-the Lamb, the Lord Jesus Christ; it is the declared will of God that all men should honour the Son as they honour the Father; for he has the same nature. (2.) Their posture: They fell down before him, gave him not an inferior sort of worship, but the most profound adoration. (3.) The instruments used in their adorations-harps and vials; the harps were the instruments of praise, the vials were full of odours or incense, which signify the prayers of the saints: prayer and praise should always go together. (4.) The matter of their song: it was suited to the new state of the church, the gospel-state introduced by the Son of God. In this new song, [1.] They acknowledge the infinite fitness and worthiness of the Lord Jesus for this great work of opening and executing the counsel and purposes of God (Rev 5:9): Thou art worthy to take the book, and to open the seals thereof, every way sufficient for the work and deserving the honour. [2.] They mention the grounds and reasons of this worthiness; and though they do not exclude the dignity of his person as God, without which he had not been sufficient for it, yet they chiefly insist upon the merit of his sufferings, which he had endured for them; these more sensibly struck their souls with thankfulness and joy. Here, First, They mention his suffering: "Thou wast slain, slain as a sacrifice, thy blood was shed." Secondly, The fruits of his sufferings. 1. Redemption to God; Christ has redeemed his people from the bondage of sin, guilt, and Satan, redeemed them to God, set them at liberty to serve him and to enjoy him. 2. High exaltation: Thou hast made us to our God kings and priests, and we shall reign on the earth, Rev 5:10. Every ransomed slave is not immediately preferred to honour; he thinks it a great favour to be restored to liberty. But when the elect of God were made slaves by sin and Satan, in every nation of the world, Christ not only purchased their liberty for them, but the highest honour and preferment, made them kings and priests-kings, to rule over their own spirits, and to overcome the world, and the evil one; and he has made them priests, given them access to himself, and liberty to offer up spiritual sacrifices, and they shall reign on the earth; they shall with him judge the world at the great day.

2. The doxology, thus begun by the church, is carried on by the angels; they take the second part, in conjunction with the church, Rev 5:11. They are said to be innumerable, and to be the attendants on the throne of God and guardians to the church; though they did not need a Saviour themselves, yet they rejoice in the redemption and salvation of sinners, and they agree with the church in acknowledging the infinite merits of the Lord Jesus as dying for sinners, that he is worthy to receive power, and riches, and wisdom, and strength, and honour, and glory, and blessing. (1.) He is worthy of that office and that authority which require the greatest power and wisdom, the greatest fund, all excellency, to discharge them aright; and, (2.) He is worthy of all honour, and glory, and blessing, because he is sufficient for the office and faithful in it.

3. This doxology, thus begun by the church, and carried on by the angels, is resounded and echoed by the whole creation, Rev 5:13. Heaven and earth ring with the high praises of the Redeemer. The whole creation fares the better for Christ. By him all things consist; and all the creatures, had they sense and language, would adore that great Redeemer who delivers the creature from that bondage under which it groans, through the corruption of men, and the just curse denounced by the great God upon the fall; that part which (by a prosopopoeia) is made for the whole creation is a song of blessing, and honour, and glory, and power, (1.) To him that sits on the throne, to God as God, or to God the Father, as the first person in the Trinity and the first in the economy of our salvation; and, (2.) To the Lamb, as the second person in the Godhead and the Mediator of the new covenant. Not that the worship paid to the Lamb is of another nature, an inferior worship, for the very same honour and glory are in the same words ascribed to the Lamb and to him that sits on the throne, their essence being the same; but, their parts in the work of our salvation being distinct they are distinctly adored. We worship and glorify one and the same God for our creation and for our redemption.

We see how the church that began the heavenly anthem, finding heaven and earth join in the concert, closes all with their Amen, and end as they began, with a low prostration before the eternal and everlasting God. Thus we have seen this sealed book passing with great solemnity from the hand of the Creator into the hand of the Redeemer.

Revelation Chapter 6

The book of the divine counsels being thus lodged in the hand of Christ, he loses no time, but immediately enters upon the work of opening the seals and publishing the contents; but this is done in such a manner as still leaves the predictions very abstruse and difficult to be understood. Hitherto the waters of the sanctuary have been as those in Ezekiel's vision, only to the ankles, or to the knees, or to the loins at least; but here they begin to be a river that cannot be passed over. The visions which John saw, the epistles to the churches, the songs of praise, in the two foregoing chapters, had some things dark and hard to be understood; and yet they were rather milk for babes than meat for strong men; but now we are to launch into the deep, and our business is not so much to fathom it as to let down our net to take a draught. We shall only hint at what seems most obvious. The prophecies of this book are divided into seven seals opened, seven trumpets sounding, and seven vials poured out. It is supposed that the opening of the seven seals discloses those providences that concerned the church in the first three centuries, from the ascension of our Lord and Saviour to the reign of Constantine; this was represented in a book rolled up, and sealed in several places, so that, when one seal was opened, you might read so far of it, and so on, till the whole was unfolded. Yet we are not here told what was written in the book, but what John saw in figures enigmatical and hieroglyphic; and it is not for us to pretend to know "the times and seasons which the Father has put in his own power." Inf this chapter six of the seven seals are opened, and the visions attending them are related; the first seal in Rev 6:1, Rev 6:2, the second seal in Rev 6:3, Rev 6:4, the third seal in Rev 6:5, Rev 6:6, the fourth seal in Rev 6:7, Rev 6:8, the fifth seal in Rev 6:9-11, the sixth seal in Rev 6:12,Rev 6:13, etc.

Revelation 6:1

Here, 1. Christ, the Lamb, opens the first seal; he now enters upon the great work of opening and accomplishing the purposes of God towards the church and the world. 2. One of the ministers of the church calls upon the apostle, with a voice like thunder, to come near, and observe what then appeared. 3. We have the vision itself, Rev 6:2. (1.) The Lord Jesus appears riding on a white horse. White horses are generally refused in war, because they make the rider a mark for the enemy; but our Lord Redeemer was sure of the victory and a glorious triumph, and he rides on the white horse of a pure but despised gospel, with great swiftness through the world. (2.) He had a bow in his hand. The convictions impressed by the word of God are sharp arrows, they reach at a distance; and, though the ministers of the word draw the bow at a venture, God can and will direct it to the joints of the harness. This bow, in the hand of Christ, abides in strength, and, like that of Jonathan, never returns empty. (3.) A crown was given him, importing that all who receive the gospel must receive Christ as a king, and must be his loyal and obedient subjects; he will be glorified in the success of the gospel. When Christ was going to war, one would think a helmet had been more proper than a crown; but a crown is given him as the earnest and emblem of victory. (4.) He went forth conquering, and to conquer. As long as the church continues militant Christ will be conquering; when he has conquered his enemies in one age he meets with new ones in another age; men go on opposing, and Christ goes on conquering, and his former victories are pledges of future victories. He conquers his enemies in his people; their sins are their enemies and his enemies; when Christ comes with power into their soul he begins to conquer these enemies, and he goes on conquering, in the progressive work of sanctification, till he has gained us a complete victory. And he conquers his enemies in the world, wicked men, some by bringing them to his foot, others by making them his footstool. Observe, From this seal opened, [1.] The successful progress of the gospel of Christ in the world is a glorious sight, worth beholding, the most pleasant and welcome sight that a good man can see in this world. [2.] Whatever convulsions and revolutions happen in the states and kingdoms of the world, the kingdom of Christ shall be established and enlarged in spite of all opposition. [3.] A morning of opportunity usually goes before a night of calamity; the gospel is preached before the plagues are poured forth. [4.] Christ's work is not all done at once. We are ready to think, when the gospel goes forth, it should carry all the world before it, but it often meets with opposition, and moves slowly; however, Christ will do his own work effectually, in his own time and way.

Revelation 6:3

The next three seals give us a sad prospect of great and desolating judgments with which God punishes those who either refuse or abuse the everlasting gospel. Though some understand them of the persecutions that befell the church of Christ, and others of the destruction of the Jews, they rather seem more generally to represent God's terrible judgments, by which he avenges the quarrel of his covenant upon those who make light of it.

I. Upon opening the second seal, to which John was called to attend, another horse appears, of a different colour from the former, a red horse, Rev 6:4. This signifies the desolating judgment of war; he that sat upon this red horse had power to take peace from the earth, and that the inhabitants of the earth should kill one another. Who this was that sat upon the red horse, whether Christ himself, as Lord of hosts, or the instruments that he raised up to conduct the war, is not clear; but this is certain, 1. That those who will not submit to the bow of the gospel must expect to be cut in sunder by the sword of divine justice. 2. That Jesus Christ rules and commands, not only in the kingdom of grace, but of providence. And, 3. That the sword of war is a dreadful judgment; it takes away peace from the earth, one of the greatest blessings, and it puts men upon killing one another. Men, who should love one another and help one another, are, in a state of war, set upon killing one another.

II. Upon opening the third seal, which John was directed to observe, another horse appears, different from the former, a black horse, signifying famine, that terrible judgment; and he that sat on the horse had a pair of balances in his hand (Rev 6:5), signifying that men must now eat their bread by weight, as was threatened (Lev 26:26), They shall deliver your bread to you by weight. That which follows in Rev 6:6, of the voice that cried, A measure of wheat for a penny, and three measures of barley for a penny, and see thou hurt not the oil and the wine, has made some expositors think this was not a vision of famine, but of plenty; but if we consider the quantity of their measure, and the value of their penny, at the time of this prophecy, the objection will be removed; their measure was but a single quart, and their penny was our sevenpence-halfpenny, and that is a large sum to give for a quart of wheat. However, it seems this famine, as all others, fell most severely upon the poor; whereas the oil and the wine, which were dainties of the rich, were not hurt; but if bread, the staff of life, be broken, dainties will not supply the place of it.

Here observe, 1. When a people loathe their spiritual food, God may justly deprive them of their daily bread. 2. One judgment seldom comes alone; the judgment of war naturally draws after it that of famine; and those who will not humble themselves under one judgment must expect another and yet greater, for when God contends he will prevail. The famine of bread is a terrible judgment; but the famine of the word is more so, though careless sinners are not sensible of it.

III. Upon opening the fourth seal, which John is commanded to observe, there appears another horse, of a pale colour. Here observe, 1. The name of the rider-Death, the king of terrors; the pestilence, which is death in its empire, death reigning over a place or nation, death on horseback, marching about, and making fresh conquests every hour. 2. The attendants or followers of this king of terrors-hell, a state of eternal misery to all those who die in their sins; and, in times of such a general destruction, multitudes go down unprepared into the valley of destruction. It is an awful thought, and enough to make the whole world to tremble, that eternal damnation immediately follows upon the death of an impenitent sinner. Observe, (1.) There is a natural as well as judicial connection between one judgment and another: war is a wasting calamity, and draws scarcity and famine after it; and famine, not allowing men proper sustenance, and forcing them to take that which is unwholesome, often draws the pestilence after it. (2.) God's quiver is full of arrows; he is never at a loss for ways and means to punish a wicked people. (3.) In the book of God's counsels he has prepared judgments for scorners as well as mercy for returning sinners. (4.) In the book of the scriptures God has published threatenings against the wicked as well as promises to the righteous; and it is our duty to observe and believe the threatenings as well as the promises.

IV. After the opening of these seals of approaching judgments, and the distinct account of them, we have this general observation, that God gave power to them over the fourth part of the earth, to kill with the sword, and with hunger, and with death, and with the beasts of the earth, Rev 6:8. He gave them power, that is, those instruments of his anger, or those judgments themselves; he who holds the winds in his hand has all public calamities at his command, and they can only go when he sends them and no further than he permits. To the three great judgments of war, famine, and pestilence, is here added the beasts of the earth, another of God's sore judgments, mentioned Eze 14:21, and mentioned here the last, because, when a nation is depopulated by the sword, famine, and pestilence, the small remnant that continue in a waste and howling wilderness encourage the wild beasts to make head against them, and they become easy prey. Others, by the beasts of the field, understand brutish, cruel, savage men, who, having divested themselves of all humanity, delight to be the instruments of the destruction of others.

Revelation 6:9

In the remaining part of this chapter we have the opening of the fifth and the sixth seals.

I. The fifth seal. Here is no mention made of any one who called the apostle to make his observation, probably because the decorum of the vision was to be observed, and each of the four living creatures had discharged its duty of a monitor before, or because the events here opened lay out of the sight, and beyond the time, of the present ministers of the church; or because it does not contain a new prophecy of any future events, but rather opens a spring of support and consolation to those who had been and still were under great tribulation for the sake of Christ and the gospel. Here observe,

1. The sight this apostle saw at the opening of the fifth seal; it was a very affecting sight (Rev 6:9): I saw under the altar the souls of those that were slain for the word of God, and for the testimony which they held. He saw the souls of the martyrs. Here observe, (1.) Where he saw them-under the altar; at the foot of the altar of incense, in the most holy place; he saw them in heaven, at the foot of Christ. Hence note, [1.] Persecutors can only kill the body, and after that there is no more that they can do; their souls live. [2.] God has provided a good place in the better world for those who are faithful to death and are not allowed a place any longer on earth. [3.] Holy martyrs are very near to Christ in heaven, they have the highest place there. [4.] It is not their own death, but the sacrifice of Christ, that gives them a reception into heaven and a reward there; they do not wash their robes in their own blood, but in the blood of the Lamb. (2.) What was the cause in which they suffered-the word of God and the testimony which they held, for believing the word of God, and attesting or confessing the truth of it; this profession of their faith they held fast without wavering, even though they died for it. A noble cause, the best that any man can lay down his life for-faith in God's word and a confession of that faith.

2. The cry he heard; it was a loud cry, and contained a humble expostulation about the long delay of avenging justice against their enemies: How long, O Lord, holy and true, dost thou not judge and avenge our blood on those that dwell on the earth? Rev 6:10. Observe, (1.) Even the spirits of just men made perfect retain a proper resentment of the wrong they have sustained by their cruel enemies; and though they die in charity, praying, as Christ did, that God would forgive them, yet they are desirous that, for the honour of God, and Christ, and the gospel, and for the terror and conviction of others, God will take a just revenge upon the sin of persecution, even while he pardons and saves the persecutors. (2.) They commit their cause to him to whom vengeance belongeth, and leave it in his hand; they are not for avenging themselves, but leave all to God. (3.) There will be joy in heaven at the destruction of the implacable enemies of Christ and Christianity, as well as at the conversion of other sinners. When Babylon falls, it will be said, Rejoice over her, O thou heaven, and you holy apostles and prophets, for God hath avenged you on her, Rev 18:20.

3. He observed the kind return that was made to this cry (Rev 6:11), both what was given to them and what was said to them. (1.) What was given to them-white robes, the robes of victory and of honour; their present happiness was an abundant recompence of their past sufferings. (2.) What was said to them-that they should be satisfied, and easy in themselves, for it would not be long ere the number of their fellow-sufferers would be fulfilled. This is a language rather suited to the imperfect state of the saints in this world than to the perfection of their state in heaven; there is no impatience, no uneasiness, no need of admonition; but in this world there is great need of patience. Observe, [1.] There is a number of Christians, known to God, who are appointed as sheep for the slaughter, set apart to be God's witnesses. [2.] As the measure of the sin of persecutors is filling up, so is the number of the persecuted martyred servants of Christ. [3.] When this number is fulfilled, God will take a just and glorious revenge upon their cruel persecutors; he will recompense tribulation to those who trouble them, and to those that are troubled full and uninterrupted rest.

II. We have here the sixth seal opened, Rev 6:12. Some refer this to the great revolutions in the empire at Constantine's time, the downfall of paganism; others, with great probability, to the destruction of Jerusalem, as an emblem of the general judgment, and destruction of the wicked, at the end of the world; and, indeed, the awful characters of this event are so much the same with those signs mentioned by our Saviour as foreboding the destruction of Jerusalem, as hardly to leave any room for doubting but that the same thing is meant in both places, though some think that event was past already. See Mat 24:29, Mat 24:30. Here observe,

1. The tremendous events that were hastening; and here are several occurrences that contribute to make that day and dispensation very dreadful:-(1.) There was a great earthquake. This may be taken in a political sense; the very foundations of the Jewish church and state would be terribly shaken, though they seemed to be as stable as the earth itself. (2.) The sun became black as sackcloth of hair, either naturally, by a total eclipse, or politically, by the fall of the chief rulers and governors of the land. (3.) The moon should become as blood; the inferior officers, or their military men, should be all wallowing in their own blood. (4.) The stars of heaven shall fall to the earth (Rev 6:13), and that as a fig-tree casteth her untimely figs, when she is shaken of a mighty wind. The stars may signify all the men of note and influence among them, though in lower spheres of activity; there should be a general desolation. (5.) The heaven should depart as a scroll when it is rolled together. This may signify that their ecclesiastical state should perish and be laid aside for ever. (6.) Every mountain and island shall be moved out of its place. The destruction of the Jewish nation should affect and affright all the nations round about, those who were highest in honour and those who seemed to be best secured; it would be a judgment that should astonish all the world. This leads to,

2. The dread and terror that would seize upon all sorts of men in that great and awful day, Rev 6:15. No authority, nor grandeur, nor riches, nor valour, nor strength, would be able to support men at that time; yea, the very poor slaves, who, one would think, had nothing to fear, because they had nothing to lose, would be all in amazement at that day. Here observe, (1.) The degree of their terror and astonishment: it should prevail so far as to make them, like distracted desperate men, call to the mountains to fall upon them, and to the hills to cover them; they would be glad to be no more seen; yea, to have no longer any being. (2.) The cause of their terror, namely, the angry countenance of him that sits on the throne, and the wrath of the Lamb. Observe, [1.] That which is matter of displeasure to Christ is so to God; they are so entirely one that what pleases or displeases the one pleases or displeases the other. [2.] Though God be invisible, he can make the inhabitants of this world sensible of his awful frowns. [3.] Though Christ be a lamb, yet he can be angry, even to wrath, and the wrath of the Lamb is exceedingly dreadful; for if the Redeemer, that appeases the wrath of God, himself be our wrathful enemy, where shall we have a friend to plead for us? Those perish without remedy who perish by the wrath of the Redeemer. [4.] As men have their day of opportunity, and their seasons of grace, so God has his day of righteous wrath; and, when that day shall come, the most stout-hearted sinners will not be able to stand before him: all these terrors actually fell upon the sinners in Judea and Jerusalem in the day of their destruction, and they will all, in the utmost degree, fall upon impenitent sinners, at the general judgment of the last day.

Revelation Chapter 7

The things contained in this chapter came in after the opening of the six seals, which foretold great calamities in the world; and before the sound of the seven trumpets, which gave notice of great corruptions arising in the church: between these comes in this comfortable chapter, which secures the graces and comforts of the people of God in times of common calamity. We have, I. An account of the restraint laid upon the winds (Rev 7:1-3). II. The sealing of the servants of God (Rev 7:4-8). III. The songs of angels and saints on this occasion (Rev 7:9-12). IV. A description of the honour and happiness of those who had faithfully served Christ, and suffered for him (Rev 7:13, etc.).

Revelation 7:1

Here we have, I. An account of the restraint laid upon the winds. By these winds we suppose are meant those errors and corruptions in religion which would occasion a great deal of trouble and mischief to the church of God. Sometimes the Holy Spirit is compared to the wind: here the spirits of error are compared to the four winds, contrary one to another, but doing much hurt to the church, the garden and vineyard of God, breaking the branches and blasting the fruits of his plantation. The devil is called the prince of the power of the air; he, by a great wind, overthrew the house of Job's eldest son. Errors are as wind, by which those who are unstable are shaken, and carried to and fro, Eph 4:14. Observe, 1. These are called the winds of the earth, because they blow only in these lower regions near the earth; heaven is always clear and free from them. 2. They are restrained by the ministry of angels, standing on the four corners of the earth, intimating that the spirit of error cannot go forth till God permits it, and that the angels minister to the good of the church by restraining its enemies. 3. Their restraint was only for a season, and that was till the servants of God were sealed in their foreheads. God has a particular care and concern for his own servants in times of temptation and corruption, and he has a way to secure them from the common infection; he first establishes them, and then he tries them; he has the timing of their trials in his own hand.

II. An account of the sealing of the servants of God, where observe, 1. To whom this work was committed-to an angel, another angel. While some of the angels were employed to restrain Satan and his agents, another angel was employed to mark out and distinguish the faithful servants of God. 2. How they were distinguished-the seal of God was set upon their foreheads, a seal known to him, and as plain as if it appeared in their foreheads; by this mark they were set apart for mercy and safety in the worst of times. 3. The number of those that were sealed, where observe, (1.) A particular account of those that were sealed of the twelve tribes of Israel-twelve thousand out of every tribe, the whole sum amounting to a hundred and forty-four thousand. In this list the tribe of Dan is omitted, perhaps because they were greatly addicted to idolatry; and the order of the tribes is altered, perhaps according as they had been more or less faithful to God. Some take these to be a select number of the Jews who were reserved for mercy at the destruction of Jerusalem; others think that time was past, and therefore it is to be more generally applied to

God's chosen remnant in the world; but, if the destruction of Jerusalem was not yet over (and I think it is hard to prove that it was), it seems more proper to understand this of the remnant of that people which God had reserved according to the election of grace, only here we have a definite number for an indefinite. (2.) A general account of those who were saved out of other nations (Rev 7:9): A great multitude, which no man could number, of all nations, and kindreds, and people, and tongues. Though these are not said to be sealed, yet they were selected by God out of all nations, and brought into his church, and there stood before the throne. Observe, [1.] God will have a greater harvest of souls among the Gentiles than he had among the Jews. More are the children of the desolate than of the married woman. [2.] The Lord knows who are his, and he will keep them safe in times of dangerous temptation. [3.] Though the church of God is but a little flock, in comparison of the wicked world, yet it is no contemptible society, but really large and to be still more enlarged.

III. We have the songs of saints and angels on this occasion, Rev 7:9-12, where observe,

1. The praises offered up by the saints (and, as it seems to me, by the Gentile believers) for the care of God in reserving so large a remnant of the Jews, and saving them from infidelity and destruction. The Jewish church prayed for the Gentiles before their conversion, and the Gentile churches have reason to bless God for his distinguishing mercy to so many of the Jews, when the rest were cut off. Here observe, (1.) The posture of these praising saints: they stood before the throne, and before the Lamb, before the Creator and the Mediator. In acts of religious worship we come nigh to God, and are to conceive ourselves as in his special presence; and we must come to God by Christ. The throne of God would be inaccessible to sinners were it not for a Mediator. (2.) Their habit: they were clothed with white robes, and had palms in their hands; they were invested with the robes of justification, holiness, and victory, and had palms in their hands, as conquerors used to appear in their triumphs: such a glorious appearance will the faithful servants of God make at last, when they have fought the good fight of faith and finished their course. (3.) Their employment: they cried with a loud voice, saying, Salvation to our God who sitteth upon the throne, and to the Lamb. This may be understood either as a hosannah, wishing well to the interest of God and Christ in the church and in the world, or as a hallelujah, giving to God and the Lamb the praise of the great salvation; both the Father and the Son are joined together in these praises; the Father contrived this salvation, the Son purchased it, and those who enjoy it must and will bless the Lord and the Lamb, and they will do it publicly, and with becoming fervour.

2. Here is the song of the angels (Rev 7:11, Rev 7:12), where observe, (1.) Their station-before the throne of God, attending on him, and about the saints, ready to serve them. (2.) Their posture, which is very humble, and expressive of the greatest reverence: They fell before the throne on their faces, and worshipped God. Behold the most excellent of all the creatures, who never sinned, who are before him continually, not only covering their faces, but falling down on their faces before the Lord! What humility then, and what profound reverence, become us vile frail creatures, when we come into the presence of God! We should fall down before him; there should be both a reverential frame of spirit and a humble behaviour in all our addresses to God (3.) Their praises. They consented to the praises of the saints, said their Amen thereto; there is in heaven a perfect harmony between the angels and saints; and then they added more of their own, saying, Blessing, and glory, and wisdom, and thanksgiving, and honour, and power, and might,

be unto our God for ever and ever. Amen. Here, [1.] They acknowledge the glorious attributes of God-his wisdom, his power, and his might. [2.] They declare that for these his divine perfections he ought to be blessed, and praised, and glorified, to all eternity; and they confirm it by their Amen. We see what is the work of heaven, and we ought to begin it now, to get our hearts tuned for it, to be much in it, and to long for that world where our praises, as well as happiness, will be perfected.

Revelation 7:13

Here we have a description of the honour and happiness of those who have faithfully served the Lord Jesus Christ, and suffered for him. Observe,

I. A question asked by one of the elders, not for his own information, but for John's instruction: ministers may learn from the people, especially from aged and experienced Christians; the lowest saint in heaven knows more than the greatest apostle in the world. Now the question has two parts:-1. What are these that are arrayed in white robes? 2. Whence came they? It seems to be spoken by way of admiration, as Sol 3:6, Who is this that cometh out of the wilderness! Faithful Christians deserve our notice and respect; we should mark the upright.

II. The answer returned by the apostle, in which he tacitly acknowledges his own ignorance, and sues to this elder for information: Thou knowest. Those who would gain knowledge must not be ashamed to own their ignorance, nor to desire instruction from any that are able to give it.

III. The account given to the apostle concerning that noble army of martyrs who stood before the throne of God in white robes, with palms of victory in their hands: and notice is taken here of, 1. The low and desolate state they had formerly been in; they had been in great tribulation, persecuted by men, tempted by Satan, sometimes troubled in their own spirits; they had suffered the spoiling of their goods, the imprisonment of their persons, yea, the loss of life itself. The way to heaven lies through many tribulations; but tribulation, how great soever, shall not separate us from the love of God. Tribulation, when gone through well, will make heaven more welcome and more glorious. 2. The means by which they had been prepared for the great honour and happiness they now enjoyed: they had washed their robes, and made them white in the blood of the Lamb,Rev 7:14. It is not the blood of the martyrs themselves, but the blood of the Lamb, that can wash away sin, and make the soul pure and clean in the sight of God. Other blood stains; this is the only blood that makes the robes of the saints white and clean. 3. The blessedness to which they are now advanced, being thus prepared for it. (1.) They are happy in their station, for they are before the throne of God night and day; and he dwells among them; they are in that presence where there is fulness of joy. (2.) They are happy in their employment, for they serve God continually, and that without weakness, drowsiness, or weariness. Heaven is a state of service, though not of suffering; it is a state of rest, but not of sloth; it is a praising delightful rest. (3.) They are happy in their freedom from all the inconveniences of this present life. [1.] From all want and sense of want: They hunger and thirst no more; all their wants are supplied, and all the uneasiness caused thereby is removed. [2.] From all sickness and pain: they shall never be scorched by the heat of the sun any more. (4.) They are happy in the love and guidance of the Lord Jesus: He shall feed them, he shall lead them to living fountains of waters, he shall put them into the possession of every thing that is pleasant and refreshing to their souls, and therefore they shall hunger and thirst no more. (5.) They are happy in being delivered from all sorrow or occasion of it: God shall wipe away all tears from their eyes. They have formerly had their sorrows, and shed many tears, both upon the account of sin and affliction; but God himself, with his own gentle and gracious hand, will wipe those tears away, and they shall return no more for ever; and they would not have been without those tears, when God comes to wipe them away. In this he deals with them as a tender father who finds his beloved child in tears, he comforts him, he wipes his eyes, and turns his sorrow into rejoicing. This should moderate the Christian's sorrow in his present state, and support him under all the troubles of it; for those that sow in tears shall reap in joy; and those that now go forth weeping, bearing precious seed, shall doubtless come again rejoicing, bringing their sheaves with them.

Revelation Chapter 8

Revelation

We have already seen what occurred upon opening six of the seals; we now come to the opening of the seventh, which introduced the sounding of the seven trumpets; and a direful scene now opens. Most expositors agree that the seven seals represent the interval between the apostle's time and the reign of Constantine, but that the seven trumpets are designed to represent the rise of antichrist, some time after the empire became Christian. In this chapter we have, I. The preface, or prelude, to the sounding of the trumpets (Rev 8:1-6). II. The sounding of four of the trumpets (Rev 8:7, etc.).

Revelation 8:1

In these verses we have the prelude to the sounding of the trumpets in several parts.

I. The opening of the last seal. This was to introduce a new set of prophetical iconisms and events; there is a continued chain of providence, one part linked to another (where one ends another begins), and, though they may differ in nature and in time, they all make up one wise, well-connected, uniform design in the hand of God.

II. A profound silence in heaven for the space of half an hour, which may be understood either, 1. Of the silence of peace, that for this time no complaints were sent up to the ear of the Lord God of sabaoth; all was quiet and well in the church, and therefore all silent in heaven, for whenever the church on earth cries, through oppression, that cry comes up to heaven and resounds there; or, 2. A silence of expectation; great things were upon the wheel of providence, and the church of God, both in heaven and earth, stood silent, as became them, to see what God was doing, according to that of Zac 2:13, Be silent, O all flesh, before the Lord, for he has risen up out of his holy habitation. And elsewhere, Be still, and know that I am God.

III. The trumpets were delivered to the angels who were to sound them. Still the angels are employed as the wise and willing instruments of divine Providence, and they are furnished with all their materials and instructions from God our Saviour. As the angels of the churches are to sound the trumpet of the gospel, the angels of heaven are to sound the trumpet of Providence, and every one has his part given him.

IV. To prepare for this, another angel must first offer incense, Rev 8:3. It is very probable that this other angel is the Lord Jesus, the high priest of the church, who is here described in his sacerdotal office, having a golden censer and much incense, a fulness of merit in his own glorious person, and this incense he was to offer up, with the prayers of all the saints, upon the golden altar of his divine nature. Observe, 1. All the saints are a praying people; none of the children of God are born dumb, a Spirit of grace is always a Spirit of adoption and supplication, teaching us to cry, Abba, Father. Psa 32:6, For this shall every one that is godly pray unto thee. 2. Times of danger should be praying times, and so should times of great expectation; both our fears and our hopes should put us upon prayer, and, where the interest of the church of God is deeply concerned, the hearts of the people of God in prayer should be greatly enlarged. 3. The prayers of the saints themselves stand in need of the incense and intercession of Christ to make them acceptable and effectual, and there is provision made by Christ for that purpose; he has his incense, his censer, and his altar; he is all himself to his people. 4. The prayers of the saints come up before God in a cloud of incense; no prayer, thus recommended, was ever denied audience or acceptance. 5. These prayers that were thus accepted in heaven produced great changes upon earth in return to them; the same angel that in his censer offered up the prayers of the saints in the same censer took of the fire of the altar, and cast it into the earth, and this presently caused strange commotions, voices, and thunderings, and lightnings, and an earthquake; these were the answers God gave to the prayers of the saints, and tokens of his anger against the world and that he would do great things to avenge himself and his people of their enemies; and now, all things being thus prepared, the angels discharge their duty.

Revelation 8:7

Observe, I. The first angel sounded the first trumpet, and the events which followed were very dismal: There followed hail and fire mingled with blood, etc., Rev 8:7. There was a terrible storm; but whether it is to be understood of a storm of heresies, a mixture of monstrous errors falling on the church (for in that age Arianism prevailed), or a storm or tempest of war falling on the civil state, expositors are not agreed. Mr. Mede takes it to be meant of the Gothic inundation that broke in upon the empire in the year 395, the same year that Theodosius died, when the northern nations, under Alaricus, king of the Goths, broke in upon the western parts of the empire. However, here we observe, 1. It was a very terrible storm-fire, and hail, and blood: a strange mixture! 2. The limitation of it: it fell on the third part of the trees, and on the third part of the grass, and blasted and burnt it up; that is, say some, upon the third part of the clergy and the third part of the laity; or, as others who take it to fall upon the civil state, upon the third part of the great men, and upon the third part of the common people, either upon the Roman empire itself, which was a third part of the then known world, or upon a third part of that empire. The most severe calamities have their bounds and limits set them by the great God.

II. The second angel sounded, and the alarm was followed, as in the first, with terrible events: A great mountain burning with fire was cast into the sea; and the third part of the sea became blood, Rev 8:8. By this mountain some understand the leader or leaders of the heretics; others, as Mr. Mede, the city of Rome, which was five times sacked by the Goths and Vandals, within the compass of 137 years; first by Alaricus, in the year 410, with great slaughter and cruelty. In these calamities, a third part of the people (called here the sea or collection of waters) were destroyed: here was still a limitation to the third part, for in the midst of judgment God remembers mercy. This storm fell heavy upon the maritime and merchandizing cities and countries of the Roman empire.

III. The third angel sounded, and the alarm had the like effects as before: There fell a great star from heaven, etc., Rev 8:10. Some take this to be a political star, some eminent governor, and they apply it to Augustulus, who was forced to resign the empire to Odoacer, in the year 480. Others take it to be an ecclesiastical star, some eminent person in the church, compared to a burning lamp, and they fix it upon Pelagius, who proved about this time a falling star, and greatly corrupted the churches of Christ. Observe, 1. Where this star fell: Upon a third part of the rivers, and upon the fountains of waters. 2. What effect it had upon them; it turned those springs and streams into wormwood, made them very bitter, that men were poisoned by them; either the laws, which are springs of civil liberty, and property, and safety, were poisoned by arbitrary power, or the doctrines of the gospel, the springs of spiritual life, refreshment, and vigour to the souls of men, were so corrupted and embittered by a mixture of dangerous errors that the souls of men found their ruin where they sought for their refreshment.

IV. The fourth angel sounded, and the alarm was followed with further calamities. Observe, 1. The nature of this calamity; it was darkness; it fell therefore upon the great luminaries of the heaven, that give light to the world-the sun, and the moon, and the stars, either the guides and governors of the church, or of the state, who are placed in higher orbs than the people, and are to dispense light and benign influences to them. 2. The limitation: it was confined to a third part of these luminaries; there was some light both of the sun by day, and of the moon and stars by night, but it was only a third part of what they had before. Without determining what is matter of controversy in these points among learned men, we rather choose to make these plain and practical remarks:-(1.) Where the gospel comes to a people, and is but coldly received, and has not its proper effects upon their hearts and lives, it is usually followed with dreadful judgments. (2.) God gives warning to men of his judgments before he sends them; he sounds an alarm by the written word, by ministers, by men's own consciences, and by the signs of the times; so that, if a people be surprised, it is their own fault. (3.) The anger of God against a people makes dreadful work among them; it embitters all their comforts, and makes even life itself bitter and burdensome. (4.) God does not in this world stir up all his wrath, but sets bounds to the most terrible judgments. (5.) Corruptions of doctrine and worship in the church are themselves great judgments, and the usual causes and tokens of other judgments coming on a people.

V. Before the other three trumpets are sounded here is solemn warning given to the world how terrible the calamities would be that should follow them, and how miserable those times and places would be on which they fell, Rev 8:13. 1. The messenger was an angel flying in the midst of heaven, as in haste, and coming on an awful errand. 2. The message was a denunciation of further and greater woe and misery than the world had hitherto endured. Here are three woes, to show how much the calamities coming should exceed those that had been already, or to hint how every one of the three succeeding trumpets should introduce its particular and distinct calamity. If less judgments do not take effect, but the church and the world grow worse under them, they must expect greater. God will be known by the judgments that he executes; and he expects, when he comes to punish the world, the inhabitants thereof should tremble before him.

Revelation Chapter 9

Revelation

In this chapter we have an account of the sounding of the fifth and sixth trumpets, the appearances that attended them, and the events that were to follow; the fifth trumpet (Rev 9:1-12), the sixth (Rev 9:13, etc.).

Revelation 9:1

Upon the sounding of this trumpet, the things to be observed are, 1. A star falling from heaven to the earth. Some think this star represents some eminent bishop in the Christian church, some angel of the church; for, in the same way of speaking by which pastors are called stars, the church is called heaven; but who this is expositors do not agree. Some understand it of Boniface the third bishop of Rome, who assumed the title of universal bishop, by the favour of the emperor Phocas, who, being a usurper and tyrant in the state, allowed Boniface to be so in the church, as the reward of his flattery. 2. To this fallen star was given the key of the bottomless pit. Having now ceased to be a minister of Christ, he becomes the antichrist, the minister of the devil; and by the permission of Christ, who had taken from him the keys of the church, he becomes the devil's turnkey, to let loose the powers of hell against the churches of Christ. 3. Upon the opening of the bottomless pit there arose a great smoke, which darkened the sun and the air. The devils are the powers of darkness; hell is the place of darkness. The devil carries on his designs by blinding the eyes of men, by extinguishing light and knowledge, and promoting ignorance and error. He first deceives men, and then destroys them; wretched souls follow him in the dark, or they durst not follow him. 4. Out of this dark smoke there came a swarm of locusts, one of the plagues of Egypt, the devil's emissaries headed by the antichrist, all the rout and rabble of antichristian orders, to promote superstition, idolatry, error, and cruelty; and these had, by the just permission of God, power to hurt those who had not the mark of God in their foreheads. 5. The hurt they were to do them was not a bodily, but a spiritual hurt. They should not in a military way destroy all by fire and sword; the trees and the grass should be untouched, and those they hurt should not be slain; it should not be a persecution, but a secret poison and infection in their souls, which should rob them of their purity, and afterwards of their peace. Heresy is a poison in the soul, working slowly and secretly, but will be bitterness in the end. 6. They had no power so much as to hurt those who had the seal of God in their foreheads. God's electing, effectual, distinguishing grace will preserve his people from total and final apostasy. 7. The power given to these factors for hell is limited in point of time: five months, a certain season, and but a short season, though how short we cannot tell. Gospel-seasons have their limits, and times of seduction are limited too. 8. Though it would be short, it would be very sharp, insomuch that those who were made to feel the malignity of this poison in their consciences would be weary of their lives, Rev 9:6. A wounded spirit who can bear? 9. These locusts were of a monstrous size and shape, Rev 9:7, Rev 9:8, etc. They were equipped for their work like horses prepared to battle. (1.) They pretended to great authority, and seemed to be assured of victory: They had crowns like gold on their heads; it was not a true, but a counterfeit authority. (2.) They had the show of wisdom and sagacity, the faces of men, though the spirit of devils. (3.) They had all the allurements of seeming beauty, to ensnare and defile the minds of men-hair like women; their way of worship was very gaudy and ornamental. (4.) Though they appeared with the tenderness of women, they had the teeth of lions, were really cruel creatures. (5.) They had the defence and protection of earthly powers-breastplates of iron. (6.) They made a mighty noise in the world; they flew about from one country to another, and the noise of their motion was like that of an army with chariots and horses. (7.) Though at first they soothed and flattered men with a fair appearance, there was a sting in their tails; the cup of their abominations contained that which, though luscious at first, would at length bite like a serpent and sting like an adder. (8.) The king and commander of this hellish squadron is here described, [1.] As an angel; so he was by nature, an angel, once one of the angels of heaven. [2.] The angel of the bottomless pit; an angel still, but a fallen angel, fallen into the bottomless pit, vastly large, and out of which there is no recovery. [3.] In these infernal regions he is a sort of prince and governor, and has the powers of darkness under his rule and command. [4.] His true name is Abaddon, Apollyon-a destroyer, for that is his business, his design, and employment, to which he diligently attends, in which he is very successful, and takes a horrid hellish pleasure; it is about this destroying work that he sends out his emissaries and armies to destroy the souls of men. And now here we have the end of one woe; and where one ends another begins.

Revelation 9:13

Here let us consider the preface to this vision, and then the vision itself.

I. The preface to this vision: A voice was heard from the horns of the golden altar, Rev 9:13, Rev 9:14. Here observe, 1. The power of the church's enemies is restrained till God gives the word to have them turned loose. 2. When nations are ripe for punishment, those instruments of God's anger that were before restrained are let loose upon them, Rev 9:14. 3. The instruments that God makes use of to punish a people may sometimes lie at a great distance from them, so that no danger may be apprehended from them. These four messengers of divine judgment lay bound in the river Euphrates, a great way from the European nations. Here the Turkish power had its rise, which seems to be the story of this vision.

II. The vision itself: And the four angels that had been bound in the great river Euphrates were now loosed, Rev 9:15, Rev 9:16. And here observe, 1. The time of their military operations and executions is limited to an hour, and a day, and a month, and a year. Prophetic characters of time are hardly to be understood by us; but in general the time is fixed to an hour, when it shall begin and when it shall end; and how far the execution shall prevail, even to a third part of the inhabitants of the earth. God will make the wrath of man praise him, and the remainder of wrath he will restrain. 2. The army that was to execute this great commission is mustered, and the number found to be of horsemen two hundred thousand thousand; but we are left to guess what the infantry must be. In general, it tells us, the armies of the Mahomedan empire should be vastly great; and so it is certain they were. 3. Their formidable equipage and appearance, Rev 9:17. As the horses were fierce, like lions, and eager to rush into the battle, so those who sat upon them were clad in bright and costly armour, with all the ensigns of martial courage, zeal, and resolution. 4. The vast havoc and desolation that they made in the Roman empire, which had now become antichristian: A third part of them were killed; they went as far as their commission suffered them, and they could go no further. 5. Their artillery, by which they made such slaughter, described by fire, smoke, and brimstone, issuing out of the mouths of their horses, and the stings that were in their tails. It is Mr. Mede's opinion that this is a prediction of great guns, those instruments of cruelty which make such destruction: he observes, These were first used by the Turks at the siege of Constantinople, and, being new and strange, were very terrible, and did great execution. However, here seems to be an allusion to what is mentioned in the former vision, that, as antichrist had his forces of a spiritual nature, like scorpions poisoning the minds of men with error and idolatry, so the Turks, who were raised up to punish the antichristian apostasy, had their scorpions and their stings too, to hurt and kill the bodies of those who had been the murderers of so many souls. 6. Observe the impenitency of the antichristian generation under these dreadful judgments (Rev 9:20); the rest of the men who were not killed repented not, they still persisted in those sins for which God was so severely punishing them, which were, (1.) Their idolatry; they would not cast away their images, though they could do them no good, could not see, nor hear, nor walk. (2.) Their murders (Rev 9:21), which they had committed upon the saints and servants of Christ. Popery is a bloody religion, and seems resolved to continue such. (3.) Their sorceries; they have their charms, and magic arts, and rites in exorcism and other things. (4.) Their fornication; they allow both spiritual and carnal impurity, and promote it in themselves and others. (5.) Their thefts; they have by unjust means heaped together a vast deal of wealth, to the injury and impoverishing of families, cities, princes, and nations. These are the flagrant crimes of antichrist and his agents; and, though God has revealed his wrath from heaven against them, they are obstinate, hardened, and impenitent, and judicially so, for they must be destroyed.

III. From this sixth trumpet we learn, 1. God can make one enemy of the church to be a scourge and plague to another. 2. He who is the Lord of hosts has vast armies at his command, to serve his own purposes. 3. The most formidable powers have limits set them, which they cannot transgress. 4. When God's judgments are in the earth, he expects the inhabitants thereof should repent of sin, and learn righteousness. 5. Impenitency under divine judgments is an iniquity that will be the ruin of sinners; for where God judges he will overcome.

Revelation Chapter 10

Revelation

This chapter is an introduction to the latter part of the prophecies of this book. Whether what is contained between this and the sounding of the seventh trumpet (Rev 11:15) be a distinct prophecy from the other, or only a more general account of some of the principal things included in the other, is disputed by our curious enquirers into these abstruse writings. However, here we have, I. A remarkable description of a very glorious angel with an open book in his hand (Rev 10:1-3). II. An account of seven thunders which the apostle heard, as echoing to the voice of this angel, and communicating some discoveries, which the apostle was not yet allowed to write (Rev 10:4). III. The solemn oath taken by him who had the book in his hand (Rev 10:5-7). IV. The charge given to the apostle, and observed by him (Rev 10:8-11).

Revelation 10:1

Here we have an account of another vision the apostle was favoured with, between the sounding of the sixth trumpet and that of the seventh. And we observe,

I. The person who was principally concerned in communicating this discovery to John-an angel from heaven, another mighty angel, who is so set forth as would induce one to think it could be no other than our Lord and Saviour Jesus Christ! 1. He was clothed with a cloud: he veils his glory, which is too great for mortality to behold; and he throws a veil upon his dispensations. Clouds and darkness are round about him. 2. A rainbow was upon his head; he is always mindful of his covenant, and, when his conduct is most mysterious, yet it is perfectly just and faithful. 3. His face was as the sun, all bright, and full of lustre and majesty, Rev 1:16. 4. His feet were as pillars of fire; all his ways, both of grace and providence, are pure and steady.

II. His station and posture: He set his right foot upon the sea and his left foot upon the earth, to show the absolute power and dominion he had over the world. And he held in his hand a little book opened, probably the same that was before sealed, but was now opened, and gradually fulfilled by him.

III. His awful voice: He cried aloud, as when a lion roareth (Rev 10:3), and his awful voice was echoed by seven thunders, seven solemn and terrible ways of discovering the mind of God.

IV. The prohibition given to the apostle, that he should not publish, but conceal what he had learned from the seven thunders, Rev 10:4. The apostle was for preserving and publishing every thing he saw and heard in these visions, but the time had not yet come.

V. The solemn oath taken by this mighty angel. 1. The manner of his swearing: He lifted up his hand to heaven, and swore by him that liveth for ever, by himself, as God often has done, or by God as God, to whom he, as Lord, Redeemer, and ruler of the world, now appeals. 2. The matter of the oath: that there shall be time no longer; either, (1.) That there shall be now no longer delay in fulfilling the predictions of this book than till the last angel should sound; then every thing should be put into speedy execution: the mystery of God shall be finished, Rev 10:7. Or, (2.) That when this mystery of God is finished time itself shall be no more, as being the measure of things that are in a mutable changing state; but all things shall be at length for ever fixed, and so time itself swallowed up in eternity.

Revelation 10:8

Here we have, I. A strict charge given to the apostle, which was, 1. That he should go and take the little book out of the hands of that mighty angel mentioned before. This charge was given, not by the angel himself who stood upon the earth, but by the same voice from heaven that in the fourth verse had lain an injunction upon him not to write what he had discerned by the seven thunders. 2. To eat the book; this part of the charge was given by the angel himself, hinting to the apostle that before he should publish what he had discovered he must more thoroughly digest the predictions, and be in himself suitably affected with them.

II. An account of the taste and relish which this little book would have, when the apostle had taken it in; at first, while in his mouth, sweet. All persons feel a pleasure in looking into future events, and in having them foretold; and all good men love to receive a word from God, of what import soever it be. But, when this book of prophecy was more thoroughly digested by the apostle, the contents would be bitter; these were things so awful and terrible, such grievous persecutions of the people of God, and such desolation made in the earth, that the foresight and foreknowledge of them would not be pleasant, but painful to the mind of the apostle: thus was Ezekiel's prophecy to him, Eze 3:3.

III. The apostle's discharge of the duty he was called to (Rev 10:10): He took the little book out of the angel's hand, and ate it up, and he found the relish to be as was told him. 1. It becomes the servants of God to digest in their own souls the messages they bring to others in his name, and to be suitably affected therewith themselves. 2. It becomes them to deliver every message with which they are charged, whether pleasing or unpleasing to men. That which is least pleasing may be most profitable; however, God's messengers must not keep back any part of the counsel of God.

IV. The apostle is made to know that this book of prophecy, which he had now taken in, was not given him merely to gratify his own curiosity, or to affect him with pleasure or pain, but to be communicated by him to the world. Here his prophetical commission seems to be renewed, and he is ordered to prepare for another embassy, to convey those declarations of the mind and will of God which are of great importance to all the world, and to the highest and greatest men in the world, and such should be read and recorded in many languages. This indeed is the case; we have them in our language, and are all obliged to attend to them, humbly to enquire into the meaning of them, and firmly to believe that every thing shall have its accomplishment in the proper time; and, when the prophecies shall be fulfilled, the sense and truth of them will appear, and the omniscience, power, and faithfulness of the great God will be adored.

Revelation Chapter 11

Revelation

In this chapter we have an account, I. Of the measuring-reed given to the apostle, to take the dimensions of the temple (Rev 11:1, Rev 11:2). II. Of the two witnesses of God (Rev 11:3-13). III. Of the sounding of the seventh trumpet, and what followed upon it (Rev 11:14, etc.).

Revelation 11:1

This prophetical passage about measuring the temple is a plain reference to what we find in Ezekiel's vision, Eze 40:3, etc. But how to understand either the one or the other is not so easy. It should seem the design of measuring the temple in the former case was in order to the rebuilding of it, and that with advantage; the design of this measurement seems to be either, 1. For the preservation of it in those times of public danger and calamity that are here foretold; or, 2. For its trial; that it may be seen how far it agrees with the standard, or pattern, in the mount; or, 3. For its reformation; that what is redundant, deficient, or changed, may be regulated according to the true model. Observe,

I. How much was to be measured. 1. The temple; the gospel church in general, whether it be so built, so constituted, as the gospel rule directs, whether it be too narrow or too large, the door too wide or too strait. 2. The altar. That which was the place of the most solemn acts of worship may be put for religious worship in general; whether the church has the true altars, both as to substance and situation: as to substance, whether they take Christ for their altar, and lay down all their offerings there; and in situation, whether the altar be in the holiest; that is, whether they worship God in the Spirit and in truth. 3. The worshippers too must be measured, whether they make God's glory their end and his word their rule, in all their acts of worship; and whether they come to God with suitable affections, and whether their conversation be as becomes the gospel.

II. What was not to be measured (Rev 11:2), and why it should be left out. 1. What was not to be measured: The court which is without the temple measure it not. Some say that Herod, in the additions made to the temple, built an outer court, and called it the court of the Gentiles. Some tell us that Adrian built the city and an outer court, and called it Aelia, and gave it to the Gentiles. 2. Why was not the outer court measured? This was no part of the temple, according to the model either of Solomon or Zerubbabel, and therefore God would have no regard to it. He would not mark it out for preservation; but as it was designed for the Gentiles, to bring pagan ceremonies and customs and to annex them to the gospel churches, so Christ abandoned it to them, to be used as they pleased; and both that and the city were trodden under foot for a certain time-forty and two months, which some would have to be the whole time of the reign of antichrist. Those who worship in the outer court are either such as worship in a false manner or with hypocritical hearts; and these are rejected of God, and will be found among his enemies. 3. From the whole observe, (1.) God will have a temple and an altar in the world, till the end of time. (2.) He has a strict regard to this temple, and observes how every thing is managed in it. (3.) Those who worship in the outer court will be rejected, and only those who worship within the veil accepted. (4.) The holy city, the visible church, is very much trampled upon in the world. But, (5.) The desolations of the church are for a limited time, and for a short time, and she shall be delivered out of all her troubles.

Revelation 11:3

In this time of treading down, God has reserved to himself his faithful witnesses, who will not fail to attest the truth of his word and worship, and the excellency of his ways. Here observe,

I. The number of these witnesses: it is but a small number and yet it is sufficient. 1. It is but small. Many will own and acknowledge Christ in times of prosperity who will desert and deny him in times of persecution; one witness, when the cause is upon trial, is worth many at other times. 2. It is a sufficient number; for in the mouth of two witnesses every cause shall be established. Christ sent out his disciples two by two, to preach the gospel. Some think these two witnesses are Enoch and Elias, who are to return to the earth for a time: others, the church of the believing Jews and that of the Gentiles: it should rather seem that they are God's eminent faithful ministers, who shall not only continue to profess the Christian religion, but to preach it, in the worst of times.

II. The time of their prophesying, or bearing their testimony for Christ. A thousand two hundred and threescore days; that is (as many think), to the period of the reign of antichrist; and, if the beginning of that interval could be ascertained, this number of prophetic days, taking a day for a year, would give us a prospect when the end shall be.

III. Their habit, and posture: they prophesy in sackcloth, as those that are deeply affected with the low and distressed state of the churches and interest of Christ in the world.

IV. How they were supported and supplied during the discharge of their great and hard work: they stood before the God of the whole earth, and he gave them power to prophesy. He made them to be like Zerubbabel and Joshua, the two olive-trees and candlestick in the vision of Zechariah, Zac 4:2, etc. God gave them the oil of holy zeal, and courage, and strength, and comfort; he made them olive-trees, and their lamps of profession were kept burning by the oil of inward gracious principles, which they received from God. They had oil not only in their lamps, but in their vessels-habits of spiritual life, light, and zeal.

V. Their security and defence during the time of their prophesying: If any attempted to hurt them, fire proceeded out of their mouths, and devoured them,Rev 11:5. Some think this alludes to Elias's calling for the fire from heaven, to consume the captains and their companies that came to seize him, Kg2 1:12. God promised the prophet Jeremiah (Jer 5:14), Behold, I will make my words in thy mouth fire, and this people shall be wood, and it shall devour them. By their praying and preaching, and courage in suffering, they shall gall and wound the very hearts and consciences of many of their persecutors, who shall go away self-condemned, and be even terrors to themselves; like Pashur, at the words of the prophet Jeremiah, Jer 20:4. They shall have that free access to God, and that interest in him, that, at their prayers, God will inflict plagues and judgments upon their enemies, as he did on Pharaoh, turning their rivers into blood, and restraining the dews of heaven, shutting heaven up, that no rain shall fall for many days, as he did at the prayers of Elias, Kg1 17:1. God has ordained his arrows for the persecutors, and is often plaguing them while they are persecuting his people; they find it hard work to kick against the pricks.

VI. The slaying of the witnesses. To make their testimony more strong, they must seal it with their blood. Here observe, 1. The time when they should be killed: When they have finished their testimony. They are immortal, they are invulnerable, till their work be done. Some think it ought to be rendered, when they were about to finish their testimony. When they had prophesied in sackcloth the greatest part of the 1260 years, then they should feel the last effect of antichristian malice. 2. The enemy that should overcome and slay them-the beast that ascendeth out of the bottomless pit. Antichrist, the great instrument of the devil, should make war against them, not only with the arms of subtle and sophistical learning, but chiefly with open force and violence; and God would permit his enemies to prevail against his witnesses for a time. 3. The barbarous usage of these slain witnesses; the malice of their enemies was not satiated with their blood and death, but pursued even their dead bodies. (1.) They would not allow them a quiet grave; their bodies were cast out in the open street, the high street of Babylon, or in the high road leading to the city. This city is spiritually called Sodom for monstrous wickedness, and Egypt for idolatry and tyranny; and here Christ in his mystical body has suffered more than in any place in the world. (2.) Their dead bodies were insulted by the inhabitants of the earth, and their death was a matter of mirth and joy to the antichristian world, Rev 11:10. They were glad to be rid of these witnesses, who by their doctrine and example had teased, terrified, and tormented the consciences of their enemies; these spiritual weapons cut wicked men to the heart, and fill them with the greatest rage and malice against the faithful.

VII. The resurrection of these witnesses, and the consequences thereof. Observe, 1. The time of their rising again; after they had lain dead three days and a half (Rev 11:11), a short time in comparison of that in which they had prophesied. Here may be a reference to the resurrection of Christ, who is the resurrection and the life. Thy dead men shall live, together with my dead body shall they arise. Or there may be a reference to the resurrection of Lazarus on the fourth day, when they thought it impossible. God's witnesses may be slain, but they shall rise again: not in their persons, till the general resurrection, but in their successors. God will revive his work, when it seems to be dead in the world. 2. The power by which they were raised: The spirit of life from God entered into them, and they stood upon their feet. God put not only life, but courage into them. God can make the dry bones to life; it is the Spirit of life from God that quickens dead souls, and shall quicken the dead bodies of his people, and his dying interest in the world. 3. The effect of their resurrection upon their enemies: Great fear fell upon them. The reviving of God's work and witnesses will strike terror into the souls of his enemies. Where there is guilt, there is fear; and a persecuting spirit, though cruel, is not a courageous, but a cowardly spirit. Herod feared John the Baptist.

VIII. The ascension of the witnesses into heaven and the consequences thereof,Rev 11:12, Rev 11:13. Observe, 1. Their ascension. By heaven we may understand either some more eminent station in the church, the kingdom of grace in this world, or a high place in the kingdom of glory above. The former seems to be the meaning: They ascended to heaven in a cloud (in a figurative, not in a literal sense) and their enemies saw them. It will be no small part of the punishment of persecutors, both in this world and at the great day, that they shall see the faithful servants of

God greatly honoured and advanced. To this honour they did not attempt to ascend, till God called them, and said, Come up hither. The Lord's witnesses must wait for their advancement, both in the church and in heaven, till God calls them; they must not be weary of suffering and service, nor too hastily grasp at the reward; but stay till their Master calls them, and then they may gladly ascend to him. 2. The consequences of their ascension-a mighty shock and convulsion in the antichristian empire and the fall of a tenth part of the city. Some refer this to the beginning of the reformation from popery, when many princes and states fell off from their subjection to Rome. This great work met with great opposition; all the western world felt a great concussion, and the antichristian interest received a great blow, and lost a great deal of ground and interest, (1.) By the sword of war, which was then drawn; and many of those who fought under the banner of antichrist were slain by it. (2.) By the sword of the Spirit: The fear of God fell upon many. They were convinced of their errors, superstition, and idolatry; and by true repentance, and embracing the truth, they gave glory to the God of heaven. Thus, when God's work and witnesses revive, the devil's work and witnesses fall before him.

Revelation 11:14

We have here the sounding of the seventh and last trumpet, which is ushered in by the usual warning and demand of attention: The second woe is past, and, behold, the third woe cometh quickly. Then the seventh angel sounded. This had been suspended for some time, till the apostle had been made acquainted with some intervening occurrences of very great moment, and worthy of his notice and observation. But what he before expected he now heard-the seventh angel sounding. Here observe the effects and consequences of this trumpet, thus sounded.

I. Here were loud and joyful acclamations of the saints and angels in heaven. Observe, 1. The manner of their adorations: they rose from their seats, and fell upon their faces, and worshipped God; they did it with reverence and humility. 2. The matter of their adorations. (1.) They thankfully recognize the right of our God and Saviour to rule and reign over all the world: The kingdoms of this world have become the kingdoms of our Lord and of his Christ, Rev 11:15. They were always so in title, both by creation and purchase. (2.) They thankfully observe his actual possession of them, and reign over them; they give him thanks because he had taken to him his great power, asserted his rights, exerted his power, and so turned title into possession. (3.) They rejoice that this his reign shall never end: He shall reign for ever and ever, till all enemies be put under his feet; none shall ever wrest the sceptre out of his hand.

II. Here were angry resentments in the world at these just appearances and actings of the power of God (Rev 11:18): The nations were angry; not only had been so, but were so still: their hearts rose up against God; they met his wrath with their own anger. It was a time when God was taking a just revenge upon the enemies of his people, recompensing tribulation to those who had troubled them. It was a time in which he was beginning to reward his people's faithful services and sufferings; and their enemies could not bear it, they fretted against God, and so increased their guilt and hastened their destruction.

III. Another consequence was the opening of the temple of God in heaven. By this may be meant that here is now a more free communication between heaven and earth, prayer and praises more freely and frequently ascending and graces and blessings plentifully descending. But it rather seems to intend the church of God on earth, a heavenly temple. It is an allusion to the various circumstances of things in the time of the first temple. Under idolatrous and wicked princes, it was shut up and neglected; but, under religious and reforming princes, it was opened and frequented. So, during the power of antichrist, the temple of God seemed to be shut up, and was so in a great degree; but now it was opened again. At this opening of it observe, 1. What was seen there: the ark of God's testament. This was in the holy of holies; in this ark the tables of the law were kept. As before Josiah's time the law of God had been lost, but was then found, so in the reign of antichrist God's law was laid aside, and made void by their traditions and decrees; the scriptures were locked up from the people, and they must not look into these divine oracles; now they are opened, now they are brought to the view of all. This was an unspeakable and invaluable privilege; and this, like the ark of the testament, was a token of the presence of God returned to his people, and his favour towards them in Jesus Christ the propitiation. 2. What was heard and felt there: Lightnings, voices, thunderings, an earthquake, and great hail. The great blessing of the reformation was attended with very awful providences; and by terrible things in righteousness God would answer those prayers that were presented in his holy temple, now opened. All the great revolutions of the world are concerted in heaven, and are the answers of the prayers of the saints.

Revelation Chapter 12

It is generally agreed by the most learned expositors that the narrative we have in this and the two following chapters, from the sounding of the seventh trumpet to the opening of the vials, is not a prediction of things to come, but rather a recapitulation and representation of things past, which, as God would have the apostle to foresee while future, he would have him to review now that they were past, that he might have a more perfect idea of them in his mind, and might observe the agreement between the prophecy and that Providence that is always fulfilling the scriptures. In this chapter we have an account of the contest between the church and antichrist, the seed of the woman and the seed of the serpent. I. As it was begun in heaven (Rev 12:1-11). II. As it was carried on in the wilderness (Rev 12:12, etc.).

Revelation 12:1

Here we see that early prophecy eminently fulfilled in which God said he would put enmity between the seed of the woman and the seed of the serpent, Gen 3:15. You will observe,

I. The attempts of Satan and his agents to prevent the increase of the church, by devouring her offspring as soon as it was born; of this we have a very lively description in the most proper images.

1. We see how the church is represented in this vision. (1.) As a woman, the weaker part of the world, but the spouse of Christ, and the mother of the saints. (2.) As clothed with the sun, the imputed righteousness of the Lord Jesus Christ. Having put on Christ, who is the Sun of righteousness, she, by her relation to Christ, is invested with honourable rights and privileges, and shines in his rays. (3.) As having the moon under her feet (that is, the world); she stands upon it, but lives above it; her heart and hope are not set upon sublunary things, but on the things that are in heaven, where her head is. (4.) As having on her head a crown of twelve stars, that is, the doctrine of the gospel preached by the twelve apostles, which is a crown of glory to all true believers. (5.) As in travail, crying out, and pained to be delivered. She was pregnant, and now in pain to bring forth a holy progeny to Christ, desirous that what was begun in the conviction of sinners might end in their conversion, that when the children were brought to the birth there might be strength to bring forth, and that she might see of the travail of her soul.

2. How the grand enemy of the church is represented. (1.) As a great red dragon-a dragon for strength and terror-a red dragon for fierceness and cruelty. (2.) As having seven heads, that is, placed on seven hills, as Rome was; and therefore it is probable that pagan Rome is here meant. (3.) As having ten horns, divided into ten provinces, as the Roman empire was by Augustus Caesar. (4.) As having seven crowns upon his head, which is afterwards expounded to be seven kings, Rev 17:10. (5.) As drawing with his tail a third part of the stars in heaven, and casting them down to the earth, turning the ministers and professors of the Christian religion out of their places and privileges and making them as weak and useless as he could. (6.) As standing before

the woman, to devour her child as soon as it should be born, very vigilant to crush the Christian religion in its birth and entirely to prevent the growth and continuance of it in the world.

II. The unsuccessfulness of these attempts against the church; for, 1. She was safely delivered of a man-child (Rev 12:5), by which some understand Christ, others Constantine, but others, with greater propriety, a race of true believers, strong and united, resembling Christ, and designed, under him, to rule the nations with a rod of iron; that is, to judge the world by their doctrine and lives now, and as assessors with Christ at the great day. 2. Care was taken of this child: it was caught up to God, and to his throne; that is, taken into his special, powerful, and immediate protection. The Christian religion has been from its infancy the special care of the great God and our Saviour Jesus Christ. 3. Care was taken of the mother as well as of the child, Rev 12:6. She fled into the wilderness, a place prepared both for her safety and her sustenance. The church was in an obscure state, dispersed; and this proved her security, through the care of divine Providence. This her obscure and private state was for a limited time, not to continue always.

III. The attempts of the dragon not only proved unsuccessful against the church, but fatal to his own interests; for, upon his endeavour to devour the man-child, he engaged all the powers of heaven against him (Rev 12:7): There was war in heaven. Heaven will espouse the quarrel of the church. Here observe,

1. The seat of this war-in heaven, in the church, which is the kingdom of heaven on earth, under the care of heaven and in the same interest.

2. The parties-Michael and his angels on one side, and the dragon and his angels on the other: Christ, the great Angel of the covenant, and his faithful followers; and Satan and all his instruments. This latter party would be much superior in number and outward strength to the other; but the strength of the church lies in having the Lord Jesus for the captain of their salvation.

3. The success of the battle: The dragon and his angels fought and prevailed not; there was a great struggle on both sides, but the victory fell to Christ and his church, and the dragon and his angels were not only conquered, but cast out; the pagan idolatry, which was a worshipping of devils, was extirpated out of the empire in the time of Constantine.

4. The triumphant song that was composed and used on this occasion, Rev 12:10, Rev 12:11. Here observe, (1.) How the conqueror is adored: Now have come salvation, strength, and the kingdom of our God, and the power of his Christ. Now God has shown himself to be a mighty God; now Christ has shown himself to be a strong and mighty Saviour; his own arm has brought salvation, and now his kingdom will be greatly enlarged and established. The salvation and strength of the church are all to be ascribed to the king and head of the church. (2.) How the conquered enemy is described. [1.] By his malice; he was the accuser of the brethren, and accused them before their God night and day; he appeared before God as an adversary to the church, continually bringing in indictments and accusations against them, whether true or false; thus he accused Job, and thus he accused Joshua the high priest, Zac 3:1. Though he hates the presence of God, yet he is willing to appear there to accuse the people of God. Let us therefore take heed that we give him no cause of accusation against us; and that, when we have sinned, we

presently go in before the Lord, and accuse and condemn ourselves, and commit our cause to Christ as our Advocate. [2.] By his disappointment and defeat: he and all his accusations are cast out, the indictments quashed, and the accuser turned out of the court with just indignation. (3.) How the victory was gained. The servants of God overcame Satan, [1.] By the blood of the Lamb, as the meritorious cause. Christ by dying destroyed him that hath the power of death, that is, the devil. [2.] By the word of their testimony, as the great instrument of war, the sword of the Spirit, which is the word of God,-by a resolute powerful preaching of the everlasting gospel, which is mighty, through God, to pull down strongholds,-and by their courage and patience in sufferings; they loved not their lives unto the death, when the love of life stood in competition with their loyalty to Christ; they loved not their lives so well but they could give them up to death, could lay them down in Christ's cause; their love to their own lives was overcome by stronger affections of another nature; and this their courage and zeal helped to confound their enemies, to convince many of the spectators, to confirm the souls of the faithful, and so contributed greatly to this victory.

Revelation 12:12

We have here an account of this war, so happily finished in heaven, or in the church, as it was again renewed and carried on in the wilderness, the place to which the church had fled, and where she had been for some time secured by the special care of her God and Saviour. Observe,

I. The warning given of the distress and calamity that should fall upon the inhabitants of the world in general, through the wrath and rage of the devil. For, though his malice is chiefly bent against the servants of God, yet he is an enemy and hater of mankind as such; and, being defeated in his designs against the church, he is resolved to give all the disturbance he can to the world in general: Woe to the inhabitants of the earth, and the sea, Rev 12:12. The rage of Satan grows so much the greater as he is limited both in place and time; when he was confined to the wilderness, and had but a short time to reign there, he comes with the greater wrath.

II. His second attempt upon the church now in the wilderness: He persecuted the woman who brought forth the man-child, Rev 12:13. Observe, 1. The care that God had taken of his church. He had conveyed her as on eagles' wings, into a place of safety provided for her, where she was to continue for a certain space of time, couched in prophetic characters, taken from Dan 7:25. 2. The continual malice of the dragon against the church. Her obscurity could not altogether protect her; the old subtle serpent, which at first lurked in paradise, now follows the church into the wilderness, and casts out a flood of water after her, to carry her away. This is thought to be meant of a flood of error and heresy, which was breathed by Arius, Nestorius, Pelagius, and many more, by which the church of God was in danger of being overwhelmed and carried away. The church of God is in more danger from heretics than from persecutors; and heresies are as certainly from the devil as open force and violence. 3. The seasonable help provided for the church in this dangerous juncture: The earth helped the woman, and opened her mouth, and swallowed up the flood, Rev 12:16. Some think we are to understand the swarms of Goths and Vandals that invaded the Roman empire, and found work for the Arian rulers, who otherwise would have been as furious persecutors as the pagan had been, and had exercised great cruelties already; but God opened a breach of war, and the flood was in a manner swallowed up thereby, and the church enjoyed some respite. God often sends the sword to avenge the quarrel of his covenant; and, when men choose new gods, then there is danger of war in the gates; intestine broils and contentions often end in the invasions of a common enemy. 4. The devil, being thus defeated in his designs upon the universal church, now turns his rage against particular persons and places; his malice against the woman pushes him on to make war with the remnant of her seed. Some think hereby are meant the Albigenses, who were first by Dioclesian driven up into barren and mountainous places, and afterwards cruelly murdered by popish rage and power, for several generations; and for no other reason than because they kept the commandments of God and held the testimony of Jesus Christ. Their fidelity to God and Christ, in doctrine, worship, and practice, was that which exposed them to the rage of Satan and his instruments; and such fidelity will expose men still, less or more, to the end of the world, when the last enemy shall be destroyed.

Revelation Chapter 13

Revelation

We have, in this chapter, a further discovery and description of the church's enemies: not other enemies than are mentioned before, but described after another manner, that the methods of their enmity may more fully appear. They are represented as two beasts; the first you have an account of (Rev 13:1-10) the second (Rev 13:11, etc.). By the first some understand Rome pagan, and by the second Rome papal; but others understand Rome papal to be represented by both these beasts, by the first in its secular power, by the second in its ecclesiastical.

Revelation 13:1

We have here an account of the rise, figure, and progress of the first beast; and observe, 1. From what situation the apostle saw this monster. He seemed to himself to stand upon the sea-shore, though it is probable he was still in a rapture; but he took himself to be in the island Patmos, but whether in the body or out of the body he could not tell. 2. Whence this beast came-out of the sea; and yet, by the description of it, it would seem more likely to be a land-monster; but the more monstrous every thing about it was the more proper an emblem it would be to set forth the mystery of iniquity and tyranny. 3. What was the form and shape of this beast. It was for the most part like a leopard, but its feet were like the feet of a bear and its mouth as the mouth of a lion; it had seven heads, and ten horns, and upon its heads the name of blasphemy: the most horrid and hideous monster! In some part of this description here seems to be an allusion to Daniel's vision of the four beasts, which represented the four monarchies, Dan 7:1-3, etc. One of these beasts was like a lion, another like a bear, and another like a leopard; this beast was a sort of composition of those three, with the fierceness, strength, and swiftness, of them all; the seven heads and the ten horns seem to design its several powers; the ten crowns, its tributary princes; the word blasphemy on its forehead proclaims its direct enmity and opposition to the glory of God, by promoting idolatry. 4. The source and spring of his authority-the dragon; he gave him his power, and seat, and great authority. He was set up by the devil, and supported by him to do his work and promote his interest; and the devil lent him all the assistance he could. 5. A dangerous wound given him, and yet unexpectedly healed, Rev 13:3. Some think that by this wounded head we are to understand the abolishing of pagan idolatry; and by the healing of the wound the introducing of the popish idolatry, the same in substance with the former, only in a new dress, and which as effectually answers the devil's design as that did. 6. The honour and worship paid to this infernal monster: All the world wondered after the beast; they all admired his power, and policy, and success, and they worshipped the dragon that gave power to the beast, and they worshipped the beast; they paid honour and subjection to the devil and his instruments, and thought there was no power able to withstand them: so great were the darkness, degeneracy, and madness of the world! 7. How he exercised his infernal power and policy: He had a mouth, speaking great things, and blasphemies; he blasphemed God, the name of God, the tabernacle of God, and all those that dwell in heaven; and he made war with the saints, and overcame them, and gained a sort of universal empire in the world. His malice was principally levelled at the God of heaven, and his heavenly attendants-at God, in making images of him that is invisible, and in worshipping them;-at the tabernacle of God, that is, say some, at the human nature of the Lord Jesus Christ, in which God dwells as in a tabernacle; this is dishonoured by their doctrine of transubstantiation, which will not suffer his body to be a true body, and will put it into the power of every priest to prepare a body for Christ;-and against those that dwell in heaven, the glorified saints, by putting them into the place of the pagan demons, and praying to them, which they are so far from being pleased with that they truly judge themselves wronged and dishonoured by it. Thus the malice of the devil shows itself against heaven and the blessed inhabitants of heaven. These are above the reach of his power. All he can do is to blaspheme them; but the saints on earth are more exposed to his cruelty, and he sometimes is permitted to triumph over them and trample upon them. 8. The limitation of the devil's power and success, and that both as to time and persons. He is limited in point of time; his reign is to continue forty-and-two months (Rev 13:5), suitable to the other prophetical characters of the reign of antichrist. He is also limited as to the persons and people that he shall entirely subject his will and power; it will be only those whose names are not written in the Lamb's book of life. Christ had a chosen remnant, redeemed by his blood, recorded in his book, sealed by his Spirit; and though the devil and antichrist might overcome their bodily strength, and take away their natural life, they could never conquer their souls, nor prevail with them to forsake their Saviour and revolt to his enemies. 9. Here is a demand of attention to what is here discovered of the great sufferings and troubles of the church, and an assurance given that when God has accomplished his work on mount Zion, his refining work, then he will turn his hand against the enemies of his people, and those who have killed with the sword shall themselves fall by the sword (Rev 13:10), and those who led the people of God into captivity shall themselves be made captives. Here now is that which will be proper exercise for the patience and faith of the saints-patience under the prospect of such great sufferings, and faith in the prospect of so glorious a deliverance.

Revelation 13:11

Those who think the first beast signifies Rome pagan by this second beast would understand Rome papal, which promotes idolatry and tyranny, but in a more soft and lamb-like manner: those that understand the first beast of the secular power of the papacy take the second to intend its spiritual and ecclesiastical powers, which act under the disguise of religion and charity to the souls of men. Here observe,

I. The form and shape of this second beast: He had two horns like a lamb, but a mouth that spoke like the dragon. All agree that this must be some great impostor, who, under a pretence of religion, shall deceive the souls of men. The papists would have it to be Apollonius Tyranaeus; but Dr. More has rejected that opinion, and fixes it upon the ecclesiastical powers of the papacy. The pope shows the horns of a lamb, pretends to be the vicar of Christ upon earth, and so to be vested with his power and authority; but his speech betrays him, for he gives forth those false doctrines and cruel decrees which show him to belong to the dragon, and not to the Lamb.

II. The power which he exercises: All the power of the former beast (Rev 13:12); he promotes the same interest, pursues the same design in substance, which is, to draw men off from worshipping the true God to worshipping those who by nature are no gods, and subject the souls and consciences of men to the will and authority of men, in opposition to the will of God. This design is promoted by the popery as well as by paganism, and by the crafty arts of popery as well as by the secular arm, both serving the interests of the devil, though in a different manner.

III. The methods by which this second beast carried on his interests and designs; they are of three sorts:-1. Lying wonders, pretended miracles, by which they should be deceived, and prevailed with to worship the former beast in this new image or shape that was now made for him; they would pretend to bring down fire from heaven, as Elias did, and God sometimes permits his enemies, as he did the magicians of Egypt, to do things that seem very wonderful, and by which unwary persons may be deluded. It is well known that the papal kingdom has been long supported by pretended miracles. 2. Excommunications, anathemas, severe censures, by which they pretend to cut men off from Christ, and cast them into the power of the devil, but do indeed deliver them over to the secular power, that they may be put to death; and thus, notwithstanding their vile hypocrisy, they are justly charged with killing those whom they cannot corrupt. 3. By disfranchisement, allowing none to enjoy natural, civil, or municipal rights, who will not worship that papal beast, that is, the image of the pagan beast. It is made a qualification for buying and selling the rights of nature, as well as for places of profit and trust, that they have the mark of the beast in their forehead and in their right hand, and that they have the name of the beast and the number of his name. It is probable that the mark, the name, and the number of the beast, may all signify the same thing-that they make an open profession of their subjection and obedience to the papacy, which is receiving the mark in their forehead, and that they oblige themselves to use all their interest, power, and endeavour, to promote the papal authority, which is receiving the mark in their right hands. We are told that pope Martin V. in his bull, added to the council of Constance, prohibits Roman catholics from suffering any heretics to dwell in their countries, or to make any bargains, use any trades, or bear any civil offices, which is a very clear interpretation of this prophecy.

IV. We have here the number of the beast, given in such a manner as shows the infinite wisdom of God, and will sufficiently exercise all the wisdom and accuracy of men: The number is the number of a man, computed after the usual manner among men, and it is 666. Whether this be the number of the errors and heresies that are contained in popery, or rather, as others, the number of the years from its rise to its fall, is not certain, much less what that period is which is described by these prophetic numbers. The most admired dissertation on this intricate subject is that of Dr. Potter, where the curious may find sufficient entertainment. It seems to me to be one of those seasons which God has reserved in his own power; only this we know, God has written Mene Tekel upon all his enemies; he has numbered their days, and they shall be finished, but his own kingdom shall endure for ever.

Revelation Chapter 14

Revelation

After an account of the great trials and sufferings which the servants of God had endured, we have now a more pleasant scene opening; the day begins now to dawn, and here we have represented, I. The Lord Jesus at the head of his faithful followers (Rev 14:1-5). II. Three angels sent successively to proclaim the fall of Babylon and the things antecedent and consequent to so great an event (Rev 14:6-13). III. The vision of the harvest (Rev 14:14, etc.).

Revelation 14:1

Here we have one of the most pleasing sights that can be viewed in this world-the Lord Jesus Christ at the head of his faithful adherents and attendants. Here observe, 1. How Christ appears: as a Lamb standing upon mount Zion. Mount Zion is the gospel church. Christ is with his church and in the midst of her in all her troubles, and therefore she is not consumed. It is his presence that secures her perseverance; he appears as a Lamb, a true Lamb, the Lamb of God. A counterfeit lamb is mentioned as rising out of the earth in the last chapter, which was really a dragon; here Christ appears as the true paschal Lamb, to show that his mediatorial government is the fruit of his sufferings, and the cause of his people's safety and fidelity. 2. How his people appear: very honourably. (1.) As to the numbers, they are many, even all who are sealed; not one of them lost in all the tribulations through which they have gone. (2.) Their distinguishing badge: they had the name of God written in their foreheads; they made a bold and open profession of their faith in God and Christ, and, this being followed by suitable actings, they are known and approved. (3.) Their congratulations and songs of praise, which were peculiar to the redeemed (Rev 14:3); their praises were loud as thunder, or as the voice of many waters; they were melodious, as of harpers; they were heavenly, before the throne of God. The song was new, suited to the new covenant, and unto that new and gracious dispensation of Providence under which they now were; and their song was a secret to others, strangers intermeddled not with their joy; others might repeat the words of the song, but they were strangers to the true sense and spirit of it. (4.) Their character and description. [1.] They are described by their chastity and purity: They are virgins. They had not defiled themselves either with corporal or spiritual adultery; they had kept themselves clean from the abominations of the antichristian generation. [2.] By their loyalty and stedfast adherence to Christ: They follow the Lamb withersoever he goes; they follow the conduct of his word, Spirit, and providence, leaving it to him to lead them into what duties and difficulties he pleases. [3.] By their former designation to this honour: These were redeemed from among men, being the first-fruits to God, and to the Lamb, Rev 14:4. Here is plain evidence of a special redemption: They were redeemed from among men. Some of the children of men are, by redeeming mercy, distinguished from others: They were the first-fruits to God, and to the Lamb, his choice ones, eminent in every grace, and the earnest of many more who should be followers of them, as they were of Christ. [4.] By their universal integrity and conscientiousness: There was no guile found in them, and they were without fault before the throne of God. They were without any prevailing guile, any allowed fault; their hearts were right with God, and, as for their human infirmities, they were freely pardoned in Christ. This is the happy remnant who attend upon the Lord Jesus as their head and Lord; he is glorified in them, and they are glorified in him.

Revelation 14:6

In this part of the chapter we have three angels or messengers sent from heaven to give notice of the fall of Babylon, and of those things that were antecedent and consequent to that great event.

I. The first angel was sent on an errand antecedent to it, and that was to preach the everlasting gospel, Rev 14:6, Rev 14:7. Observe, 1. The gospel is an everlasting gospel; it is so in its nature, and it will be so in its consequences. Though all flesh be grass, the word of the Lord endureth for ever. 2. It is a work fit for an angel to preach this everlasting gospel; such is the dignity, and such is the difficulty of that work! And yet we have this treasure in earthen vessels. 3. The everlasting gospel is of great concern to all the world; and, as it is the concern of all, it is very much to be desired that it should be made known to all, even to every nation, and kindred, and tongue, and people. 4. The gospel is the great means whereby men are brought to fear God, and to give glory to him. Natural religion is not sufficient to keep up the fear of God, nor to secure to him glory from men; it is the gospel that revives the fear of God, and retrieves his glory in the world. 5. When idolatry creeps into the churches of God, it is by the preaching of the gospel, attended by the power of the Holy Spirit, that men are turned from idols to serve the living God, as the Creator of the heaven, and the earth, and the sea, and the fountains of waters, Rev 14:7. To worship any God besides him who created the world is idolatry.

II. The second angel follows the other, and proclaims the actual fall of Babylon. The preaching of the everlasting gospel had shaken the foundations of antichristianism in the world, and hastened its downfall. By Babylon is generally understood Rome, which was before called Sodom and Egypt, for wickedness and cruelty, and is now first called Babylon, for pride and idolatry. Observe, 1. What God has fore-ordained and foretold shall be done as certainly as if it were done already. 2. The greatness of the papal Babylon will not be able to prevent her fall, but will make it more dreadful and remarkable. 3. The wickedness of Babylon, in corrupting, debauching, and intoxicating the nations round about her, will make her fall just and will declare the righteousness of God in her utter ruin, Rev 14:8. Her crimes are recited as the just cause of her destruction.

III. A third angel follows the other two, and gives warning to all of that divine vengeance which would overtake all those that obstinately adhered to the antichristian interest after God had thus proclaimed its downfall, Rev 14:9, Rev 14:10. If after this (this threatening denounced against Babylon, and in part already executed) any should persist in their idolatry, professing subjection to the beast and promoting his cause, they must expect to drink deep of the wind of the wrath of God; they shall be for ever miserable in soul and body; Jesus Christ will inflict this punishment upon them, and the holy angels will behold it and approve of it. Idolatry, both pagan and papal, is a damning sin in its own nature, and will prove fatal to those who persist in it, after fair warning given by the word of Providence; those who refuse to come out of Babylon, when thus called, and resolve to partake of her sins, must receive of her plagues; and the guilt and ruin of such incorrigible idolaters will serve to set forth the excellency of the patience and obedience of the saints. These graces shall be rewarded with salvation and glory. When the treachery and rebellion of others shall be punished with everlasting destruction, then it will be said, to the honour of the faithful (Rev 14:12): Here is the patience of the saints; you have before seen their patience exercised, now you see it rewarded.

Revelation 14:13

Here we have the vision of the harvest and vintage, introduced with a solemn preface. Observe,

I. The preface, Rev 14:13. Here note, 1. Whence this prophecy about the harvest came: it came down from heaven, and not from men, and therefore it is of certain truth and great authority. 2. How it was to be preserved and published-by writing; it was to be a matter of record, that the people of God might have recourse to it for their support and comfort upon all occasions. 3. What it principally intended, and that is, to show the blessedness of all the faithful saints and servants of God, both in death and after death: Blessed are the dead that die in the Lord from henceforth, etc. Here observe, (1.) The description of those that are and shall be blessed-such as die in the Lord, either die in the cause of Christ, or rather die in a state of vital union with Christ, such as are found in Christ when death comes. (2.) The demonstration of this blessedness: They rest from their labours, and their works do follow them. [1.] They are blessed in their rest; they rest from all sin, temptation, sorrow, and persecution. There the wicked cease from troubling, there the weary are at rest. [2.] They are blessed in their recompence: Their works follow them; they do not go before them as their title, or price of purchase, but follow them as their evidence of having lived and died in the Lord; and the memory of them will be pleasant, and the reward glorious, far above the merit of all their services and sufferings. [3.] They are happy in the time of their dying, when they have lived to see the cause of God reviving, the peace of the church returning, and the wrath of God falling upon their idolatrous cruel enemies. Such times are good times to die in; they have Simeon's desire: Now, Lord, let thou thy servant depart in peace, for mine eyes have seen thy salvation. And all this is ratified and confirmed by the testimony of the Spirit witnessing with their spirits and with the written word.

II. We have the vision itself, represented by a harvest and a vintage.

1. By a harvest (Rev 14:14, Rev 14:15), an emblem that sometimes signifies the cutting down of the wicked, when ripe for ruin, by the judgments of God, and sometimes the gathering in of the righteous, when ripe for heaven, by the mercy of God. This seems rather to represent God's judgments against the wicked: and here observe,

(1.) The Lord of the harvest-one so like unto the Son of man that he was the same, even the Lord Jesus, who is described, [1.] By the chariot in which he sat-a white cloud, a cloud that had a bright side turned to the church, how dark soever it might be to the wicked. [2.] By the ensign of his power: On his head was a golden crown, authority to do all that he did and whatsoever he would do. [3.] By the instrument of his providences: In his hand a sharp sickle. [4.] By the solicitations he had from the temple to perform this great work. What he did, he was desired to do by his people; and, though he was resolved to do it, he would for this thing be sought unto by them, and so it should be in return to their prayers.

(2.) The harvest-work, which is, to thrust the sickle into the corn, and reap the field. The sickle is the sword of God's justice; the field is the world; reaping is cutting the inhabitants of the earth down and carrying them off.

(3.) The harvest-time; and this is when the corn is ripe, when the measure of the sin of men is filled up, and they are ripe for destruction. The most inveterate enemies of Christ and his church are not destroyed till by their sin they are ripe for ruin, and then he will spare them no longer; he will thrust in his sickle, and the earth shall be reaped.

2. By a vintage, Rev 14:17. Some think that these two are only different emblems of the same judgment; others that they refer to distinct events of providence before the end of all things. Observe, (1.) To whom this vintage-work was committed-to an angel, another angel that came out from the altar, that is, from the holiest of all in heaven. (2.) At whose request this vintage-work was undertaken: it was, as before, at the cry of an angel out of the temple, the ministers and churches of God on earth. (3.) The work of the vintage, which consists of two parts:-[1.] The cutting off, and gathering, the clusters of the vine, which were now ripe and ready, fully ripe, Rev 14:18. [2.] Casting these grapes into the wine-press (Rev 14:19); here we are told, First, What was the wine-press: it was the wrath of God, the fire of his indignation, some terrible calamity, very probably the sword, shedding the blood of the wicked. Secondly, Where was the place of the wine-press-without the city, where the army lay that came against Babylon. Thirdly, The quantity of the wine, that is, of the blood that was drawn forth by this judgment: it was, for depth, up to the horses' bridles, and, for breadth and length, a thousand and six hundred furlongs (Rev 14:20); that is, say some, 200 Italian miles, which is thought to be the measure of the holy land, and may be meant of the patrimony of the holy see, encompassing the city of Rome. But here we are left of doubtful conjectures. Perhaps this great event has not yet had its accomplishment, but the vision is for an appointed time; and therefore, though it may seem to tarry, we are to wait for it. But who shall live when the Lord does this?

Revelation Chapter 15

Revelation

Hitherto, according to the judgment of very eminent expositors, God had represented to his servant, John, I. The state of the church under the pagan powers, in the six seals opened; and then, II. The state of the church under the papal powers, in the vision of the six trumpets that began to sound upon the opening of the seventh seal: and then is inserted. III. A more general and brief account of the past, present, and future state of the church, in the little book, etc. He now proceeds, IV. To show him how antichrist should be destroyed, by what steps that destruction should be accomplished, in the vision of the seven vials. This chapter contains an awful introduction or preparation for the pouring out of the vials, in which we have, 1. A sight of those angels in heaven who were to have the execution of this great work, and with what acclamations of joy the heavenly hosts applauded the great design (Rev 15:1-4). 2. A sight of these angels coming out of heaven to receive those vials which they were to pour out, and the great commotions this caused in the world (Rev 15:5, etc.).

Revelation 15:1

Here we have the preparation of matters for the pouring out of the seven vials, which was committed to seven angels; and observe how these angels appeared to the apostle-in heaven; it was in a wonderful manner, and that upon account, 1. Of the work they had to do, which was to finish the destruction of antichrist. God was now about to pour out his seven last plagues upon that interest; and, as the measure of Babylon's sins was filled up, they should now find the full measure of his vindictive wrath. 2. The spectators and witnesses of this their commission: all that had gotten the victory over the beast, etc. These stood on a sea of glass, representing this world, as some think, a brittle thing, that shall be broken to pieces; or, as others, the gospel covenant, alluding to the brazen sea in the temple, in which the priests were to wash (the faithful servants of God stand upon the foundation of the righteousness of Christ); or, as others, the Red Sea, that stood as it were congealed while the Israelites went through; and, the pillar of fire reflecting light upon the waters, they would seem to have fire mingled with them; and this to show that the fire of God's wrath against Pharaoh and his horses should dissolve the congealed waters, and destroy them thereby, to which there seems to be an allusion by their singing the song of Moses, in which, (1.) They extol the greatness of God's works, and the justice and truth of his ways, both in delivering his people and destroying their enemies. They rejoiced in hope, and the near prospect they had of this, though it was not yet accomplished. (2.) They call upon all nations to render unto God the fear, glory, and worship, due to such a discovery of his truth and justice: Who shall not fear thee? Rev 15:4.

Revelation 15:5

Observe, I. How these angels appeared-coming out of heaven to execute their commission: The temple of the tabernacle of the testimony in heaven was opened, Rev 15:5. Here is an allusion to the holiest of all the tabernacle and temple, where was the mercy-seat, covering the ark of the testimony, where the high priest made intercession, and God communed with his people, and heard their prayers. Now by this, as it is here mentioned, we may understand, 1. That, in the judgments God was now about to execute upon the antichristian interest, he was fulfilling the prophecies and promises of his word and covenant, which were there always before him, and of which he was ever mindful. 2. That in this work he was answering the prayers of the people, which were offered to him by their great high priest. 3. That he was herein avenging the quarrel of his own Son, and our Saviour Jesus Christ, whose offices and authority had been usurped, his name dishonoured, and the great designs of his death opposed, by antichrist and his adherents. 4. That he was opening a wider door of liberty for his people to worship him in numerous solemn assemblies, without the fear of their enemies.

II. How they were equipped and prepared for their work. Observe, 1. Their array: They were clothed with pure and white linen, and had their breasts girded with golden girdles, Rev 15:6. This was the habit of the high priests when they went in to enquire of God, and came out with an answer from him. This showed that these angels were acting in all things under the divine appointment and direction, and that they were going to prepare a sacrifice to the Lord, called the supper of the great God, Rev 19:17. The angels are the ministers of divine justice, and they do every thing in a pure and holy manner. 2. Their artillery, what it was, and whence they received it; their artillery, by which they were to do this great execution, was seven vials filled with the wrath of God; they were armed with the wrath of God against his enemies. The meanest creature, when it comes armed with the anger of God, will be too hard for any man in the world; but much more an angel of God. This wrath of God was not to be poured out all at once, but was divided into seven parts, which should successively fall upon the antichristian party. Now from whom did they receive these vials? From one of the four living creatures, one of the ministers of the true church, that is, in answer to the prayers of the ministers and people of God, and to avenge their cause, in which the angels are willingly employed.

III. The impressions these things made upon all who stood near the temple: they were all, as it were, wrapt up in clouds of smoke, which filled the temple, from the glorious and powerful presence of God; so that no man was able to enter into the temple, till the work was finished. The interests of antichrist were so interwoven with the civil interests of the nations that he could not be destroyed without giving a great shock to all the world; and the people of God would have but little rest and leisure to assemble themselves before him, while this great work was a doing. For the present, their sabbaths would be interrupted, ordinances of public worship intermitted, and all thrown into a general confusion. God himself was now preaching to the church and to all the world, by terrible things in righteousness; but, when this work was done, then the churches would have rest, the temple would be opened, and the solemn assemblies gathered, edified, and multiplied. The greatest deliverances of the church are brought about by awful and astonishing steps of Providence.

Revelation Chapter 16

In this chapter we have an account of the pouring forth of these vials that were filled with the wrath of God. They were poured out upon the whole antichristian empire, and on every thing appertaining to it. I. Upon the earth (Rev 16:2). II. Upon the sea (Rev 16:3). III. Upon the rivers and fountains of water (Rev 16:4). Here the heavenly hosts proclaim and applaud the righteousness of the judgments of God. IV. The fourth vial was poured out on the sun (Rev 16:8). V. The fifth on the seat of the beast. VI. The sixth on the river Euphrates. VII. The seventh in the air, upon which the cities of the nations fell, and great Babylon came in remembrance before God.

Revelation 16:1

We had in the foregoing chapter the great and solemn preparation that was made for the pouring out of the vials; now we have the performance of that work. Here observe,

I. That, though every thing was made ready before, yet nothing was to be put in execution without an immediate positive order from God; and this he gave out of the temple, answering the prayers of his people, and avenging their quarrel.

II. No sooner was the word of command given than it was immediately obeyed; no delay, no objection made. We find that some of the best men, as Moses and Jeremiah, did not so readily come in and comply with the call of God to their work; but the angels of God excel not only in strength, but in a readiness to do the will of God. God says, Go your ways, and pour out the vials, and immediately the work is begun. We are taught to pray that the will of God may be done on earth as it is done in heaven. And now we enter upon a series of very terrible dispensations of Providence, of which it is difficult to give the certain meaning or to make the particular application. But in the general it is worth our observation that,

1. We have here a reference and allusion to several of the plagues of Egypt, such as the turning of their waters into blood, and smiting them with boils and sores. Their sins were alike, and so were their punishments.

2. These vials have a plain reference to the seven trumpets, which represented the rise of antichrist; and we learn hence that the fall of the church's enemies shall bear some resemblance to their rise, and that God can bring them down in such ways as they chose to exalt themselves. And the fall of antichrist shall be gradual; as Rome was not built in one day, so neither shall it fall in one day, but it falls by degrees; it shall fall so as to rise no more.

3. The fall of the antichristian interest shall be universal. Every thing that any ways belonged to them, or could be serviceable to them, the premises and all their appurtenances, are put into the writ for destruction: their earth, their air, their sea, their rivers, their cities, all consigned over to

ruin, all accursed for the sake of the wickedness of that people. Thus the creation groans and suffers through the sins of men. Now we proceed to,

(1.) The first angel who poured out his vial, Rev 16:2. Observe, [1.] Where it fell-upon the earth; that is, say some, upon the common people; others upon the body of the Romish clergy, who were the basis of the papacy, and of an earthly spirit, all carrying on earthly designs. [2.] What it produced-noisome and grievous sores on all who had the mark of the beast. They had marked themselves by their sin; now God marks them out by his judgments. This sore, some think, signifies some of the first appearances of Providence against their state and interest which gave them great uneasiness, as it discovered their inward distemper and was a token of further evil; the plague-tokens appeared.

(2.) The second angel poured out his vial; and here we see, [1.] Where it fell-upon the sea; that is, say some, upon the jurisdiction and dominion of the papacy; others upon the whole system of their religion, their false doctrines, their corrupt glosses, their superstitious rites, their idolatrous worship, their pardons, indulgences, a great conflux of wicked inventions and institutions, by which they maintain a trade and traffic advantageous to themselves, but injurious to all who deal with them. [2.] What it produced: It turned the sea into blood, as the blood of a dead man, and every living soul died in the sea. God discovered not only the vanity and falsehood of their religion, but the pernicious and deadly nature of it-that the souls of men were poisoned by that which was pretended to be the sure means of their salvation.

(3.) The next angel poured out his vial; and we are told, [1.] Where it fell-upon the rivers, and upon the fountains of waters; that is, say some very learned men, upon their emissaries, and especially the Jesuits, who, like streams, conveyed the venom and poison of their errors and idolatries from the spring-head through the earth. [2.] What effect it had upon them: It turned them into blood; some think it stirred up Christian princes to take a just revenge upon those that had been the great incendiaries of the world, and had occasioned the shedding of the blood of armies and of martyrs. The following doxology (Rev 16:5, Rev 16:6) favours this sense. The instrument that God makes use of in this work is here called the angel of the waters, who extols the righteousness of God in this retaliation: They have shed the blood of thy saints, and thou hast given them blood to drink, for they are worthy, to which another angel answered by full consent, Rev 16:7.

Revelation 16:8

In these verses we see the work going on in the appointed order. The fourth angel poured out his vial, and that fell upon the sun; that is, say some, upon some eminent prince of the popish communion, who should renounce their false religion a little while before his utter downfall; and some expect it will be the German emperor. And now what will be the consequence of this? That sun which before cherished them with warm and benign influences shall now grow hot against these idolaters, and shall scorch them. Princes shall use their power and authority to suppress them, which yet will be so far from bringing them to repentance, that it will cause them to curse God and their king, and look upward, throwing out their blasphemous speeches against the God of heaven; they will be hardened to their ruin. The fifth angel poured out his vial, Rev 16:10. And observe, 1. Where this fell-upon the seat of the beast, upon Rome itself, the mystical

Babylon, the head of the antichristian empire. 2. What effect it had there: The whole kingdom of the beast was full of darkness and distress. That very city which was the seat of their policy, the source of all their learning, and all their knowledge, and all their pomp and pleasure, now becomes a source of darkness, and pain, and anguish. Darkness was one of the plagues of Egypt, and it is opposed to lustre and honour, and so forebodes the contempt and scorn to which the antichristian interest should be exposed. Darkness is opposed to wisdom and penetration, and forbodes the confusion and folly which the idolaters should discover at that time. It is opposed to pleasure and joy, and so signifies their anguish and vexation of Spirit, when their calamities thus came upon them.

Revelation 16:12

The sixth angel poured out his vial; and observe,

I. Where it fell-upon the great river Euphrates. Some take it literally, for the place where the Turkish power and empire began; and they think this is a prophecy of the destruction of the Turkish monarchy and of idolatry, which they suppose will be effected about the same time with that of the papacy, as another antichrist, and that thereby a way shall be made for the conveniency of the Jews, those princes of the east. Others take it for the river Tiber; for, as Rome is mystical Babylon, Tiber is mystical Euphrates. And when Rome shall be destroyed her river and merchandise must suffer with her.

II. What did this vial produce? 1. The drying up of the river, which furnished the city with wealth, provisions, and all sorts of accommodations. 2. A way is hereby prepared for the kings of the east. The idolatry of the church of Rome had been a great hindrance both to the conversion of the Jews, who have been long cured of their inclination to idols, and of the Gentiles, who are hardened in their idolatry by seeing that which so much symbolizes with it among those called Christians. It is therefore very probable that the downfall of popery, removing these obstructions, will open a way for both the Jews and other eastern nations to come into the church of Christ. And, if we suppose that Mahomedism shall fall at the same time, there will be still a more open communication between the western and eastern nations, which may facilitate the conversion of the Jews, and of the fulness of the Gentiles. And when this work of God appears, and is about to be accomplished, no wonder if it occasion another consequence, which is, 3. The last effort of the great dragon; he is resolved to have another push for it, that, if possible, he may retrieve the ruinous posture of his affairs in the world. He is now rallying his forces, recollecting all his spirits, to make one desperate sally before all be lost. This is occasioned by the pouring out of the sixth vial. Here observe, (1.) The instruments he makes use of to engage the powers of the earth in his cause and quarrel: Three unclean spirits like frogs come forth, one out of the mouth of the dragon, another out of the mouth of the beast, and a third out of the mouth of the false prophet. Hell, the secular power of antichrist, and the ecclesiastical power, would combine to send their several instruments, furnished with hellish malice, with worldly policy, and with religious falsehood and deceit; and these would muster up the devil's forces for a decisive battle. (2.) The means these instruments would use to engage the powers of earth in this war. They would work pretended miracles, the old stratagem of him whose coming is after the working of Satan, with all power, and signs, and lying wonders, and with all deceivableness of unrighteousness,Th2 2:9, Th2 2:10. Some think that a little before the fall of antichrist the popish pretence of power to work miracles will be revived and will very much amuse and deceive the world. (3.) The field of battle-a place called Armageddon; that is, say some, the mount of Megiddo, near to which, by a stream issuing thence, Barak overcame Sisera, and all the kings in alliance with him, Jdg 5:19. And in the valley of Megiddo Josiah was slain. This place had been famous for two events of a very different nature, the former very happy for the church of God, the latter very unhappy; but it shall now be the field of the last battle in which the church shall be engaged, and she shall be victorious. This battle required time to prepare for it, and therefore the further account of it is suspended till we come to the nineteenth chapter, Rev 19:19, Rev 19:20. (4.) The warning which God gives of this great and decisive trial, to engage his people to prepare for it,Rev 16:15. It would be sudden and unexpected, and therefore Christians should be clothed, and armed, and ready for it, that they might not be surprised and ashamed. When God's cause comes to be tried, and his battles to be fought, all his people shall be ready to stand up for his interest and be faithful and valiant in his service.

Revelation 16:17

Here we have an account of the seventh and last angel pouring forth his vial, contributing his part towards the accomplishment of the downfall of Babylon, which was the finishing stroke. And here, as before, observe,

I. Where this plague fell-on the air, upon the prince of the power of the air, that is, the devil. His powers were restrained, his policies confounded; he was bound in God's chain: the sword of God was upon his eye and upon his arm; for he, as well as the powers of the earth, is subject to the almighty power of God. He had used all possible means to preserve the antichristian interest, and to prevent the fall of Babylon-all the influence that he has upon the minds of men, blinding their judgments and perverting them, hardening their hearts, raising their enmity to the gospel as high as could be. But now here is a vial poured out upon his kingdom, and he is not able to support his tottering cause and interest any longer.

II. What it produced, 1. A thankful voice from heaven, pronouncing that now the work was done. The church triumphant in heaven saw it, and rejoiced; the church militant on earth saw it, and became triumphant. It is finished. 2. A mighty commotion on the earth-an earthquake, so great as never was before, shaking the very centre, and this ushered in by the usual concomitants of thunder and lightnings. 3. The fall of Babylon, which was divided into three parts, called the cities of the nations (Rev 16:19); having had rule over the nations, and taken in the idolatry of the nations, incorporating into her religion something of the Jewish, something of the pagan, and something of the Christian religion, she was as three cities in one. God now remembered this great and wicked city. Though for some time he seemed to have forgotten her idolatry and cruelty, yet now he gives unto her the cup of the wine of the fierceness of his wrath. And this downfall extended further than to the seat of antichrist; it reached from the centre to the circumference; and every island and every mountain, that seemed by nature and situation the most secured, were carried away in the deluge of this ruin.

III. How the antichristian party were affected with it. Though it fell upon them as a dreadful storm, as if the stones of the city, tossed up into the air, came down upon their heads, like hailstones of a talent weight each, yet they were so far from repenting that they blasphemed that

God who thus punished them. Here was a dreadful plague of the heart, a spiritual judgment more dreadful and destructive than all the rest. Observe, 1. The greatest calamities that can befall men will not bring them to repentance without the grace of God working with them. 2. Those that are not made better by the judgments of God are always the worse for them. 3. To be hardened in sin and enmity against God by his righteous judgments is a certain token of utter destruction.

Revelation Chapter 17

Revelation

This chapter contains another representation of those things that had been revealed before concerning the wickedness and ruin of antichrist. This antichrist had been before represented as a beast, and is now described as a great whore. And here, I. The apostle is invited to see this vile woman (Rev 17:1, Rev 17:2). II. He tells us what an appearance she made (Rev 17:3-6). III. The mystery of it is explained to him (Rev 17:7-12). And, IV. Her ruin foretold (Rev 17:13, etc.).

Revelation 17:1

Here we have a new vision, not as to the matter of it, for that is contemporary with what came under the three last vials; but as to the manner of description, etc. Observe, 1. The invitation given to the apostle to take a view of what was here to be represented: Come hither, and I will show thee the judgment of the great whore, etc., Rev 17:1. This is a name of great infamy. A whore [in this passage] is one that is married, and has been false to her husband's bed, has forsaken the guide of her youth, and broken the covenant of God. She had been a prostitute to the kings of the earth, whom she had intoxicated with the wine of her fornication. 2. The appearance she made: it was gay and gaudy, like such sort of creatures: She was arrayed in purple, and scarlet colour, and decked with gold, and precious stones, and pearls, Rev 17:4. Here were all the allurements of worldly honour and riches, pomp and pride, suited to sensual and worldly minds. 3. Her principal seat and residence-upon the beast that had seven heads and ten horns; that is to say, Rome, the city on seven hills, infamous for idolatry, tyranny, and blasphemy. 4. Her name, which was written on her forehead. It was the custom of impudent harlots to hang out signs, with their names, that all might know what they were. Now in this observe, (1.) She is named from her place of residence-Babylon the great. But, that we might not take it for the old Babylon literally so called, we are told there is a mystery in the name; it is some other great city resembling the old Babylon. (2.) She is named from her infamous way and practice; not only a harlot, but a mother of harlots, breeding up harlots, and nursing and training them up to idolatry, and all sorts of lewdness and wickedness-the parent and nurse of all false religion and filthy conversation. 5. Her diet: she satiated herself with the blood of the saints and martyrs of Jesus. She drank their blood with such greediness that she intoxicated herself with it; it was so pleasant to her that she could not tell when she had had enough of it: she was satiated, but never satisfied.

Revelation 17:7

Here we have the mystery of this vision explained. The apostle wonders at the sight of this woman: the angel undertakes to open this vision to him, it being the key of the former visions; and he tells the apostle what was meant by the beast on which the woman sat; but it is so explained as still to need further explanation. 1. This beast was, and is not, and yet is; that is, it was a seat of idolatry and persecution; and is not, that is, not in the ancient form, which was pagan; and yet it is, it is truly the seat of idolatry and tyranny, though of another sort and form. It ascends out of the bottomless pit (idolatry and cruelty are the issue and product of hell), and it shall return thither and go into perdition. 2. This beast has seven heads, which have a double signification. (1.) Seven mountains-the seven hills on which Rome stands; and (2.) Seven kings-seven sorts of government. Rome was governed by kings, consuls, tribunes, decemviri, dictators, emperors who were pagan, and emperors who were Christian. Five of these were extinct when this prophecy was written; one was then in being, that is, the pagan emperor; and the other, that is, the Christian emperor, was yet to come, Rev 17:10. This beast, the papacy, makes an eighth governor, and sets up idolatry again. 3. This beast had ten horns; which are said to be ten kings which have as yet received no kingdoms; as yet, that is, as some, shall not rise up till the Roman empire be broken in pieces; or, as others, shall not rise up till near the end of antichrist's reign, and so shall reign but as it were one hour with her, but shall for that time be very unanimous and very zealous in that interest, and entirely devoted to it, divesting themselves of their prerogatives and revenues (things so dear to princes), out of an unaccountable fondness for the papacy.

Revelation 17:14

Here we have some account of the downfall of Babylon, to be more fully described in the following chapter.

I. Here is a war begun between the beast and his followers, and the Lamb and his followers. The beast and his army, to an eye of sense, appear much stronger than the Lamb and his army: one would think an army with a lamb at the head of them could not stand before the great red dragon. But,

II. Here is a victory gained by the Lamb: The Lamb shall overcome. Christ must reign till all enemies be put under his feet; he will be sure to meet with many enemies, and much opposition, but he will also be sure to gain the victory.

III. Here is the ground or reason of the victory assigned; and this is taken, 1. From the character of the Lamb: He is King of kings and Lord of lords. He has, both by nature and by office, supreme dominion and power over all things; all the powers of earth and hell are subject to his check and control. 2. From the character of his followers: They are called, and chosen, and faithful. They are called out by commission to this warfare; they are chosen and fitted for it, and they will be faithful in it. Such an army, under such a commander, will at length carry all the world before them.

IV. The victory is justly aggrandized. 1. By the vast multitude who paid obedience and subjection to the beast and to the whore. She sat upon (that is, presided over) many waters; and these waters were so many multitudes of people, and nations, of all languages; yea, she reigned not only over kingdoms, but over the kings, and they were her tributaries and vassals, Rev 17:15, Rev 17:18. 2. By the powerful influence which God hereby showed he had over the minds of great men. Their hearts were in his hand, and he turned them as he pleased; for, (1.) It was of God, and to fulfil his will, that these kings agreed to give their kingdom unto the beast; they were judicially blinded and hardened to do so. And, (2.) It was of God that afterwards their hearts were turned against the whore, to hate her, and to make her desolate and naked, and to eat her flesh, and burn her with fire; they shall at length see their folly, and how they have been bewitched and enslaved by the papacy, and, out of a just resentment, shall not only fall off from

Rome, but shall be made the instruments of God's providence in her destruction.

Revelation Chapter 18

Revelation

We have here, I. An angel proclaiming the fall of Babylon (Rev 18:1, Rev 18:2). II. Assigning the reasons of her fall (Rev 18:3). III. Giving warning to all who belonged to God to come out of her (Rev 18:4, Rev 18:5), and to assist in her destruction (Rev 18:6-8). IV. The great lamentation made for her by those who had been large sharers in her sinful pleasures and profits (Rev 18:9-19). V. The great joy that there would be among others at the sight of her irrecoverable ruin (Rev 18:20, etc.).

Revelation 18:1

The downfall and destruction of Babylon form an event so fully determined in the counsels of God, and of such consequence to his interests and glory, that the visions and predictions concerning it are repeated. 1. Here is another angel sent from heaven, attended with great power and lustre, Rev 18:1. He had not only light in himself, to discern the truth of his own prediction, but to inform and enlighten the world about that great event; and not only light to discern it, but power to accomplish it. 2. This angel publishes the fall of Babylon, as a thing already come to pass; and this he does with a mighty strong voice, that all might hear the cry, and might see how well this angel was pleased to be the messenger of such tidings. Here seems to be an allusion to the prediction of the fall of pagan Babylon (Isa 21:9), where the word is repeated as it is here: has fallen, has fallen. Some have thought a double fall is hereby intended, first her apostasy, and then her ruin; and they think the words immediately following favour their opinion; She has become the habitation of devils, and the hold of every foul spirit, and the cage of every unclean and hateful bird, Rev 18:2. But this is also borrowed from Isa 21:9, and seems to describe not so much her sin of entertaining idols (which are truly called devils) as her punishment, it being a common notion that unclean spirits, as well as ominous and hateful birds, used to haunt a city or house that lay in its ruins. 3. The reason of this ruin is declared (Rev 18:3); for, though God is not obliged to give any account of his matters, yet he is pleased to do so, especially in those dispensations of providence that are most awful and tremendous. The wickedness of Babylon had been very great; for she had not only forsaken the true God herself, and set up idols, but had with great art and industry drawn all sorts of men into the spiritual adultery, and by her wealth and luxury had retained them in her interest. 4. Fair warning is given to all that expect mercy from God, that they should not only come out of her, but be assisting in her destruction, Rev 18:4, Rev 18:5. Here observe, (1.) God may have a people even in Babylon, some who belong to the election of grace. (2.) God's people shall be called out of Babylon, and called effectually. (3.) Those that are resolved to partake with wicked men in their sins must receive of their plagues. (4.) When the sins of a people reach up to heaven, the wrath of God will reach down to the earth. (5.) Though private revenge is forbidden, yet God will have his people act under him, when called to it, in pulling down his and their inveterate and implacable enemies, Rev 18:6. (6.) God will proportion the punishment of sinners to the measure of their wickedness, pride, and security, Rev 18:7. (7.) When destruction comes on a people suddenly, the surprise is a great aggravation of their misery, Rev 18:8.

Revelation 18:9

Here we have,

I. A doleful lamentation made by Babylon's friends for her fall; and here observe,

1. Who are the mourners, namely, those who had been bewitched by her fornication, those who had been sharers in her sensual pleasures, and those who had been gainers by her wealth and trade-the kings and the merchants of the earth: the kings of the earth, whom she had flattered into idolatry by allowing them to be arbitrary and tyrannical over their subjects, while they were obsequious to her; and the merchants, that is, those who trafficked with her for indulgences, pardons, dispensations, and preferments; these will mourn, because by this craft they got their wealth.

2. What was the manner of their mourning. (1.) They stood afar off, they durst not come nigh her. Even Babylon's friends will stand at a distance from her fall. Though they had been partakers with her in her sins, and in her sinful pleasures and profits, they were not willing to bear a share in her plagues. (2.) They made a grievous outcry: Alas! alas! that great city, Babylon, that mighty city! (3.) They wept, and cast dust upon their heads, Rev 18:19. The pleasures of sin are but for a season, and they will end in dismal sorrow. All those who rejoice in the success of the church's enemies will share with them in their downfall; and those who have most indulged themselves in pride and pleasure are the least able to bear calamities; their sorrows will be as excessive as their pleasure and jollity were before.

3. What was the cause of their mourning; not their sin, but their punishment. They did not lament their fall into idolatry, and luxury, and persecution, but their fall into ruin-the loss of their traffic and of their wealth and power. The spirit of antichrist is a worldly spirit, and their sorrow is a mere worldly sorrow; they did not lament for the anger of God, that had now fallen upon them, but for the loss of their outward comfort. We have a large schedule and inventory of the wealth and merchandise of this city, all which was suddenly lost (Rev 18:12, Rev 18:13), and lost irrecoverably (Rev 18:14): All things which were dainty and goodly have departed from thee, and thou shalt find them no more at all. The church of God may fall for a time, but she shall rise again; but the fall of Babylon will be an utter overthrow, like that of Sodom and Gomorrah. Godly sorrow is some support under affliction, but mere worldly sorrow adds to the calamity.

II. An account of the joy and triumph there was both in heaven and earth at the irrecoverable fall of Babylon: while her own people were bewailing her, the servants of God were called to rejoice over her, Rev 18:20. Here observe, 1. How universal this joy would be: heaven and earth, angels and saints, would join in it; that which is matter of rejoicing to the servants of God in this world is matter of rejoicing to the angels in heaven. 2. How just and reasonable; and that, (1.) Because the fall of Babylon was an act of God's vindictive justice. God was then avenging his people's cause. They had committed their cause to him to whom vengeance belongs, and now the year of recompence had come for the controversies of Zion; and, though they did not take pleasure in the miseries of any, yet they had reason to rejoice in the discoveries of the glorious justice of God. (2.) Because it was an irrecoverable ruin. This enemy should never molest them any more, and of this they were assured by a remarkable token (Rev 18:21): An angel from heaven took up a stone like a great millstone, and cast it into the sea, saying, "Thus shall Babylon be thrown down with violence, and be found no more at all; the place shall be no longer habitable by man, no work shall be done there, no comfort enjoyed, no light seen there, but utter darkness and desolation, as the reward of her great wickedness, first in deceiving the nations with her sorceries, and secondly in destroying and murdering those whom she could not deceive," Rev 18:24. Such abominable sins deserved so great a ruin.

Revelation Chapter 19

Revelation

In this chapter we have, I. A further account of the triumphant song of angels and saints for the fall of Babylon (Rev 19:1-4). II. The marriage between Christ and the church proclaimed and perfected (Rev 19:5-10). III. Another warlike expedition of the glorious head and husband of the church, with the success of it (Rev 19:10, etc.).

Revelation 19:1

The fall of Babylon being fixed, finished, and declared to be irrecoverable in the foregoing chapter, this begins with a holy triumph over her, in pursuance of the order given forth: Rejoice over her, thou heaven, and you holy apostles and prophets, Rev 18:20. They now gladly answer the call; and here you have, 1. The form of their thanksgiving, in that heavenly and most comprehensive word, Alleluia, praise you the Lord: with this they begin, with this they go on, and with this they end (Rev 19:4); their prayers are now turned into praises, their hosannas end in halleluias. 2. The matter of their thanksgiving: they praise him for the truth of his word, and the righteousness of his providential conduct, especially in this great event-the ruin of Babylon, which had been a mother, nurse, and nest of idolatry, lewdness, and cruelty (Rev 19:2), for which signal example of divine justice they ascribe salvation, and glory, and honour, and power, unto our God. 3. The effect of these their praises: when the angels and saints cried Alleluia, her fire burned more fiercely and her smoke ascended for ever and ever, Rev 19:3. The surest way to have our deliverances continued and completed is to give God the glory of what he has done for us. Praising God for what we have is praying in the most effectual manner for what is yet further to be done for us; the praises of the saints blow up the fire of God's wrath against the common enemy. 4. The blessed harmony between the angels and the saints in this triumphant song, Rev 19:4. The churches and their ministers take the melodious sound from the angels, and repeat it; falling down, and worshipping God, they cry, Amen, Alleluia.

Revelation 19:5

The triumphant song being ended, and epithalamium, or marriage-song, begins,Rev 19:6. Here observe,

I. The concert of heavenly music. The chorus was large and loud, as the voice of many waters and of mighty thunderings. God is fearful in praises. There is no discord in heaven; the morning stars sing together; no jarring string, nor key untuned, but pure and perfect melody.

II. The occasion of this song; and that is the reign and dominion of that omnipotent God who has redeemed his church by his own blood, and is now in a more public manner betrothing her to himself: The marriage of the Lamb has come, Rev 19:7. Some think this refers to the conversion of the Jews, which they suppose will succeed the fall of Babylon; others, to the general resurrection: the former seems more probable. Now, 1. You have here a description of the bride, how she appeared; not in the gay and gaudy dress of the mother of harlots, but in fine linen, clean and white, which is the righteousness of saints; in the robes of Christ's righteousness, both imputed for justification and imparted for sanctification-the stola, the white robe of absolution, adoption, and enfranchisement, and the white robe of purity and universal holiness. She had washed her robes and made them white in the blood of the Lamb; and these her nuptial ornaments she did not purchase by any price of her own, but received them as the gift and grant of her blessed Lord. 2. The marriage-feast, which, though not particularly described (as Mat 22:4), yet is declared to be such as would make all those happy who were called to it, so called as to accept the invitation, a feast made up of the promises of the gospel, the true sayings of God, Rev 19:9. These promises, opened, applied, sealed, and earnested by the Spirit of God, in holy eucharistical ordinances, are the marriage-feast; and the whole collective body of all those who partake of this feast is the bride, the Lamb's wife; they eat into one body, and drink into one Spirit, and are not mere spectators or guests, but coalesce into the espoused party, the mystical body of Christ. 3. The transport of joy which the apostle felt in himself at this vision. He fell down at the feet of the angel, to worship him, supposing him to be more than a creature, or having his thoughts at the present overpowered by the vehemency of his affections. Here observe, (1.) What honour he offered to the angel: He fell at his feet, to worship him; this prostration was a part of external worship, it was a posture of proper adoration. (2.) How the angel refused it, and this was with some resentment: "See thou do it not; have a care what thou doest, thou art doing a wrong thing." (3.) He gave a very good reason for his refusal: "I am thy fellow-servant, and of thy brethren which have the testimony of Jesus-I am a creature, thine equal in office, though not in nature; I, as an angel and messenger of God, have the testimony of Jesus, a charge to be a witness for him and to testify concerning him, and thou, as an apostle, having the Spirit of prophecy, hast the same testimony to give in; and therefore we are in this brethren and fellow-servants." (4.) He directs him to the true and only object of religious worship; namely, God: "Worship God, and him alone." This fully condemns both the practice of the papists in worshipping the elements of bread and wine, and saints, and angels, and the practice of those Socinians and Arians who do not believe that Christ is truly and by nature God, and yet pay him religious worship; and this shows what wretched fig-leaves all their evasions and excuses are which they offer in their own vindication: they stand hereby convicted of idolatry by a messenger from heaven.

Revelation 19:11

No sooner was the marriage solemnized between Christ and his church by the conversion of the Jews than the glorious head and husband of the church is called out to a new expedition, which seems to be the great battle that was to be fought at Armageddon, foretold Rev 16:16. And here observe,

I. The description of the great Commander, 1. By the seat of his empire; and that is heaven; his throne is there, and his power and authority are heavenly and divine. 2. His equipage: he is again described as sitting on a white horse, to show the equity of the cause, and certainty of success. 3. His attributes: he is faithful and true to his covenant and promise, he is righteous in all his judicial and military proceedings, he has a penetrating insight into all the strength and stratagems of his enemies, he has a large and extensive dominion, many crowns, for he is King of kings, and Lord of lords. 4. His armour; and that is a vesture dipped in blood, either his own blood, by which he purchased this mediatorial power, or the blood of his enemies, over whom he has always prevailed. 5. His name: The Word of God, a name that none fully knows but himself, only this we know, that this Word was God manifest in the flesh; but his perfections are incomprehensible by any creature.

II. The army which he commands (Rev 19:14), a very large one, made up of many armies; angels and saints followed his conduct, and resembled him in their equipage, and in their armour of purity and righteousness-chosen, and called, and faithful.

III. The weapons of his warfare-A sharp sword proceeding from his mouth (Rev 19:15), with which he smites the nations, either the threatenings of the written word, which now he is going to execute, or rather his word of command calling on his followers to take a just revenge on his and their enemies, who are now put into the wine-press of the wrath of God, to be trodden under foot by him.

IV. The ensigns of his authority, his coat of arms-a name written on his vesture and thigh, King of kings, and Lord of lords, asserting his authority and power, and the cause of the quarrel, Rev 19:16.

V. An invitation given to the fowls of heaven, that they should come and see the battle, and share in the spoil and pillage of the field (Rev 19:17, Rev 19:18), intimating that this great decisive engagement should leave the enemies of the church a feast for the birds of prey, and that all the world should have cause to rejoice in the issue of it.

VI. The battle joined. The enemy falls on with great fury, headed by the beast, and the kings of the earth; the powers of earth and hell gathered, to make their utmost effort, Rev 19:19.

VII. The victory gained by the great and glorious head of the church: The beast and the false prophet, the leaders of the army, are taken prisoners, both he who led them by power and he who led them by policy and falsehood; these are taken and cast into the burning lake, made incapable of molesting the church of God any more; and their followers, whether officers or common soldiers, are given up to military execution, and made a feast for the fowls of heaven. Though the divine vengeance will chiefly fall upon the beast, and the false prophet, yet it will be no excuse to those who fight under their banner that they only followed their leaders and obeyed their command; since they would fight for them, they must fall and perish with them. Be wise now therefore, O you kings, be instructed, you rulers of the earth; kiss the Son, lest he be angry, and you perish from the way, Psa 2:10, Psa 2:12.

Revelation Chapter 20

Revelation

This chapter is thought by some to be the darkest part of all this prophecy: it is very probable that the things contained in it are not yet accomplished; and therefore it is the wiser way to content ourselves with general observations, rather than to be positive and particular in our explications of it. Here we have an account, I. Of the binding of Satan for a thousand years (Rev 20:1-3). II. The reign of the saints with Christ for the same time (Rev 20:4-6). III. Of the loosing of Satan, and the conflict of the church with Gog and Magog (Rev 20:7-10). IV. Of the day of judgment (Rev 20:11, etc.).

Revelation 20:1

We have here, I. A prophecy of the binding of Satan for a certain term of time, in which he should have much less power and the church much more peace than before. The power of Satan was broken in part by the setting up of the gospel kingdom in the world; it was further reduced by the empire's becoming Christian; it was yet further broken by the downfall of the mystical Babylon; but still this serpent had many heads, and, when one is wounded, another has life remaining in it. Here we have a further limitation and diminution of his power. Observe, 1. To whom this work of binding Satan is committed-to an angel from heaven. It is very probable that this angel is no other than the Lord Jesus Christ; the description of him will hardly agree with any other. He is one who has power to bind the strong man armed, to cast him out, and to spoil his goods; and therefore must be stronger than he. 2. The means he makes use of in this work: he has a chain and a key, a great chain to bind Satan, and the key of the prison in which he was to be confined. Christ never wants proper powers and instruments to break the power of Satan, for he has the powers of heaven and the keys of hell. 3. The execution of this work, Rev 20:2, Rev 20:3. (1.) He laid hold on the dragon, that old serpent, which is the devil, and Satan. Neither the strength of the dragon, nor the subtlety of the serpent, was sufficient to rescue him out of the hands of Christ; he caught hold, and kept his hold. And, (2.) He cast him into the bottomless pit, cast him down with force, and with a just vengeance, to his own place and prison, from which he had been permitted to break out, and disturb the churches, and deceive the nations; now he is brought back to that prison, and there laid in chains. (3.) He is shut up, and a seal set upon him. Christ shuts, and none can open; he shuts by his power, seals by his authority; and his lock and seal even the devils themselves cannot break open. (4.) We have the term of this confinement of Satan-a thousand years, after which he was to be loosed again for a little season. The church should have a considerable time of peace and prosperity, but all her trials were not yet over.

II. An account of the reign of the saints for the same space of time in which Satan continued bound (Rev 20:4-6), and here observe,

1. Who those were that received such honour-those who had suffered for Christ, and all who had faithfully adhered to him, not receiving the mark of the beast, nor worshipping his image; all who had kept themselves clear of pagan and papal idolatry.

2. The honour bestowed upon them. (1.) They were raised from the dead, and restored to life. This may be taken either literally or figuratively; they were in a civil and political sense dead, and had a political resurrection; their liberties and privileges were revived and restored. (2.) Thrones, and power of judgment, were given to them; they were possessed of great honour, and interest, and authority, I suppose rather of a spiritual than of a secular nature. (3.) They reigned with Christ a thousand years. Those who suffer with Christ shall reign with Christ; they shall reign with him in his spiritual and heavenly kingdom, in a glorious conformity to him in wisdom, righteousness, and holiness, beyond what had been known before in the world. This is called the first resurrection, which none but those who have served Christ and suffered for him shall be favoured with. As for the wicked, they shall not be raised up and restored to their power again, till Satan be let loose; this may be called a resurrection, as the conversion of the Jews is said to be life from the dead.

3. The happiness of these servants of God is declared. (1.) They are blessed and holy, Rev 20:6. None can be blessed but those that are holy; and all that are holy shall be blessed. These were holy as a sort of first-fruits to God in this spiritual resurrection, and as such blessed by him. (2.) They are secured from the power of the second death. We know something of what the first death is, and it is awful; but we know not what this second death is. It must be much more dreadful; it is the death of the soul, eternal separation from God. The Lord grant we may never know what it is by experience. Those who have had experience of a spiritual resurrection are saved from the power of the second death.

III. An account of the return of the church's troubles, and another mighty conflict, very sharp, but short and decisive. Observe, 1. The restraints laid for a long time on Satan are at length taken off. While this world lasts, Satan's power in it will not be wholly destroyed; it may be limited and lessened, but he will have something still to do for the disturbance of the people of God. 2. No sooner is Satan let loose than he falls to his old work, deceiving the nations, and so stirring them up to make a war with the saints and servants of God, which they would never do if he had not first deceived them. They are deceived both as to the cause they engage in (they believe it to be a good cause when it is indeed a very bad one), and as to the issue: they expect to be successful, but are sure to lose the day. 3. His last efforts seem to be the greatest. The power now permitted to him seems to be more unlimited than before. He had now liberty to beat up for his volunteers in all the four quarters of the earth, and he raised a mighty army, the number of which was as the sand of the sea, Rev 20:8. 4. We have the names of the principal commanders in this army under the dragon-Gog and Magog. We need not be too inquisitive as to what particular powers are meant by these names, since the army was gathered from all parts of the world. These names are found in other parts of scripture. Magog we read of in Gen 10:2. He was one of the sons of Japheth, and peopled the country called Syria, from which his descendants spread into many other parts. Of Gog and Magog together we only read in Eze 38:2, a prophecy whence this in Revelation borrows many of its images. 5. We have the march and military disposition of this formidable army (Rev 20:9.): They went up on the breadth of the earth, and compassed the camp of the saints about, and the beloved city, that is, the spiritual Jerusalem, in which the most precious interests of the people of God are lodged, and therefore to them a beloved city. The army of the saints is described as drawn forth out of the city, and lying under the walls of it, to defend it; they were encamped about Jerusalem: but the army of the enemy was so much superior to that of the church that they compassed them and their city about. 6. You have an account of the battle, and the issue of this war: Fire came down from God out of heaven, and devoured the enemy. Thus the ruin of Gog and Magog is foretold (Eze 38:22), I will rain upon him and upon his bands an overflowing rain, and great hailstones, and fire and brimstone. God would, in an extraordinary and more immediate manner, fight this last and decisive battle for his people, that the victory might be complete and the glory redound to himself. 7. The doom and punishment of the grand enemy, the devil: he is now cast into hell, with his two great officers, the beast and the false prophet, tyranny and idolatry, and that not for any term of time, but to be there tormented night and day, for ever and ever.

Revelation 20:11

The utter destruction of the devil's kingdom very properly leads to an account of the day of judgment, which will determine every man's everlasting state; and we may be assured there will be a judgment when we see the prince of this world is judged, Joh 16:11. This will be a great day, the great day, when all shall appear before the judgment-seat of Christ. The Lord help us firmly to believe this doctrine of the judgment to come. It is a doctrine that made Felix tremble. Here we have a description of it, where observe, 1. We behold the throne, and tribunal of judgment, great and white, very glorious and perfectly just and righteous. The throne of iniquity, that establishes wickedness by a law, has no fellowship with this righteous throne and tribunal. 2. The appearance of the Judge, and that is the Lord Jesus Christ, who then puts on such majesty and terror that the earth and the heaven flee from his face, and there is no place found for them; there is a dissolution of the whole frame of nature, Pe2 3:10. 3. The persons to be judged (Rev 20:12): The dead, small and great; that is, young and old, low and high, poor and rich. None are so mean but they have some talents to account for, and none so great as to avoid the jurisdiction of this court; not only those that are found alive at the coming of Christ, but all who have died before; the grave shall surrender the bodies of men, hell shall surrender the souls of the wicked, the sea shall surrender the many who seemed to have been lost in it. 4. The rule of judgment settled: The books were opened. What books? The books of God's omniscience, who is greater than our consciences, and knows all things (there is a book of remembrance with him both for good and bad); and the book of the sinner's conscience, which, though formerly secret, will now be opened. And another book shall be opened-the book of the scriptures, the statute-book of heaven, the rule of life. This book is opened as containing the law, the touchstone by which the hearts and lives of men are to be tried. This book determines matter of right; the other books give evidence of matters of fact. Some, by the other book, called the book of life, understand the book of God's eternal counsels; but that does not seem to belong to the affair of judgment: in eternal election God does not act judicially, but with absolute sovereign freedom. 5. The cause to be tried; and that is, the works of men, what they have done and whether it be good or evil. By their works men shall be justified or condemned; for though God knows their state and their principles, and looks chiefly at these, yet, being to approve himself to angels and men as a righteous God, he will try their principles by their practices, and so will be justified when he speaks and clear when he judges. 6. The issue of the trial and judgment; and this will be according to the evidence of fact, and rule of judgment. All those who have made a covenant with death, and an agreement with hell, shall then be condemned with their infernal confederates, cast with them into the lake of fire, as not being entitled to eternal life, according to the rules of life laid down in the scripture; but those whose names are written in that book (that is, those that are justified and acquitted by the gospel) shall then be justified and acquitted by the Judge, and shall enter into eternal life, having nothing more to fear from death, or hell, or wicked men; for these are all destroyed together. Let it be our great concern to see on what terms we stand with our Bibles, whether they justify us or condemn us now; for the Judge of all will proceed by that rule. Christ shall judge the secrets of all men according to the gospel. Happy are those who have so ordered and stated their cause according to the gospel as to know beforehand that they shall be justified in the great day of the Lord!

Revelation Chapter 21

Hitherto the prophecy of this book has presented to us a very remarkable mixture of light and shade, prosperity and adversity, mercy and judgment, in the conduct of divine Providence towards the church in the world: now, at the close of all, the day breaks, and the shadows flee away; a new world now appears, the former having passed away. Some are willing to understand all that is said in these last two chapters of the state of the church even here on earth, in the glory of the latter days; but others, more probably, take it as a representation of the perfect and triumphant state of the church in heaven. Let but the faithful saints and servants of God wait awhile, and they shall not only see, but enjoy, the perfect holiness and happiness of that world. In this chapter you have, I. An introduction to the vision of the new Jerusalem (Rev 21:1-9). II. The vision itself (Rev 21:10, etc.)

Revelation 21:1

We have here a more general account of the happiness of the church of God in the future state, by which it seems most safe to understand the heavenly state.

I. A new world now opens to our view (Rev 21:1): I saw a new heaven and a new earth; that is, a new universe; for we suppose the world to be made up of heaven and earth. By the new earth we may understand a new state for the bodies of men, as well as a heaven for their souls. This world is not now newly created, but newly opened, and filled with all those who were the heirs of it. The new heaven and the new earth will not then be distinct; the very earth of the saints, their glorified bodies, will now be spiritual and heavenly, and suited to those pure and bright mansions. To make way for the commencement of this new world, the old world, with all its troubles and commotions, passed away.

II. In this new world the apostle saw the holy city, the new Jerusalem, coming down from heaven, not locally, but as to its original: this new Jerusalem is the church of God in its new and perfect state, prepared as a bride adorned for her husband, beautified with all perfection of wisdom and holiness, meet for the full fruition of the Lord Jesus Christ in glory.

III. The blessed presence of God with his people is here proclaimed and admired: I heard a great voice out of heaven, saying, Behold, the tabernacle of God is with men, etc., Rev 21:3. Observe, 1. The presence of God with his church is the glory of the church. 2. It is matter of wonder that a holy God should ever dwell with any of the children of men. 3. The presence of God with his people in heaven will not be interrupted as it is on earth, but he will dwell with them continually. 4. The covenant, interest, and relation, that there are now between God and his people, will be filled up and perfected in heaven. They shall be his people; their souls shall be assimilated to him, filled with all the love, honour, and delight in God which their relation to him requires, and this will constitute their perfect holiness; and he will be their God: God himself will be their God; his immediate presence with them, his love fully manifested to them, and his glory put upon them, will be their perfect happiness; then he will fully answer the character of the relation on his part, as they shall do on their part.

IV. This new and blessed state will be free from all trouble and sorrow; for, 1. All the effects of former trouble shall be done away. They have been often before in tears, by reason of sin, of affliction, of the calamities of the church; but now all tears shall be wiped away; no signs, no remembrance of former sorrows shall remain, any further than to make their present felicity the greater. God himself, as their tender Father, with his own kind hand, shall wipe away the tears of his children; and they would not have been without those tears when God shall come and wipe them away. 2. All the causes of future sorrow shall be for ever removed: There shall be neither death nor pain; and therefore no sorrow nor crying; these are things incident to that state in which they were before, but now all former things have passed away.

V. The truth and certainty of this blessed state are ratified by the word and promise of God, and ordered to be committed to writing, as matter of perpetual record, Rev 21:5, Rev 21:6. The subject-matter of this vision is so great, and of such great importance to the church and people of God, that they have need of the fullest assurances of it; and God therefore from heaven repeats and ratifies the truth thereof. Besides, many ages must pass between the time when this vision was given forth and the accomplishment of it, and many great trials must intervene; and therefore God would have it committed to writing, for perpetual memory, and continual use to his people. Observe, 1. The certainty of the promise averred: These words are faithful and true; and it follows, It is done, is as sure as if it were done already. We may and ought to take God's promise as present payment; if he has said that he makes all things new, it is done. 2. He gives us his titles of honour as a pledge or surety of the full performance, even those titles of Alpha and Omega, the beginning and the end. As it was his glory that he gave the rise and beginning to the world and to his church, it will be his glory to finish the work begin, and not to leave it imperfect. As his power and will were the first cause of all things, his pleasure and glory are the last end, and he will not lose his design; for then he would no longer be the Alpha and Omega. Men may begin designs which they can never bring to perfection; but the counsel of God shall stand, and he will do all his pleasure. 3. The desires of his people towards this blessed state furnish another evidence of the truth and certainty of it. They thirst after a state of sinless perfection and the uninterrupted enjoyment of God, and God has wrought in them these longing desires, which cannot be satisfied with any thing else, and therefore would be the torment of the soul if they were disappointed but it would be inconsistent with the goodness of God, and his love to his people, to create in them holy and heavenly desires, and then deny them their proper satisfaction; and therefore they may be assured that, when they have overcome their present difficulties, he will give them of the fountain of the water of life freely.

VI. The greatness of this future felicity is declared and illustrated, 1. By the freeness of it-it is the free gift of God: He gives of the water of life freely; this will not make it less but more grateful to his people. 2. The fulness of it. The people of God then lie at the fountain-head of all blessedness: they inherit all things (Rev 21:7); enjoying God, they enjoy all things. He is all in all. 3. By the tenure and title by which they enjoy this blessedness-by right of inheritance, as the sons of God, a title of all others the most honourable, as resulting from so near and endeared a relation to God himself, and the most sure and indefeasible, that can no more cease than the relation from which it results. 4. By the vastly different state of the wicked. Their misery helps to illustrate the glory and blessedness of the saints, and the distinguishing goodness of God towards them, Rev 21:8. Here observe, (1.) The sins of those who perish, among which are first mentioned their cowardliness and unbelief. The fearful lead the van in this black list. They durst not encounter the difficulties of religion, and their slavish fear proceeded from their unbelief; but those who were so dastardly as not to dare to take up the cross of Christ, and discharge their duty to him, were yet so desperate as to run into all manner of abominable wickedness-murder, adultery, sorcery, idolatry, and lying. (2.) Their punishment: They have their part in the lake that burns with fire and brimstone, which is the second death. [1.] They could not burn at a stake for Christ, but they must burn in hell for sin. [2.] They must die another death after their natural death; the agonies and terrors of the first death will consign them over to the far greater terrors and agonies of eternal death, to die and to be always dying. [3.] This misery will be their proper part and portion, what they have justly deserved, what they have in effect chosen, and what they have prepared themselves for by their sins. Thus the misery of the damned will illustrate the blessedness of those that are saved, and the blessedness of the saved will aggravate the misery of those that are damned.

Revelation 21:9

We have already considered the introduction to the vision of the new Jerusalem in a more general idea of the heavenly state; we now come to the vision itself, where observe,

I. The person that opened the vision to the apostle-one of the seven angels, that had the seven vials full of the seven last plagues, Rev 21:9. God has a variety of work and employment for his holy angels. Sometimes they are to sound the trumpet of divine Providence, and give fair warning to a careless world; sometimes they are to pour out the vials of God's anger upon impenitent sinners; and sometimes to discover things of a heavenly nature to those that are the heirs of salvation. They readily execute every commission they receive from God; and, when this world shall be at an end, yet the angels shall be employed by the great God in proper pleasant work to all eternity.

II. The place from which the apostle had this glorious view and prospect. He was taken, in ecstasy, into a high mountain. From such situations men usually have the most distinct views of adjacent cities. Those who would have clear views of heaven must get as near heaven as they can, into the mount of vision, the mount of meditation and faith, whence, as from the top of Pisgah, they may behold the goodly land of the heavenly Canaan.

III. The subject-matter of the vision-the bride, the Lamb's wife (Rev 21:10); that is, the church of God in her glorious, perfect, triumphant state, under the resemblance of Jerusalem, having the glory of God shining in its lustre, as uxor splendit radiis mariti-the bride comely through the comeliness put on her by her husband; glorious in her relation to Christ, in his image now perfected in her, and in his favour shining upon her. And now we have a large description of the church triumphant under the emblem of a city, far exceeding in riches and splendour all the cities of this world; and this new Jerusalem is here represented to us both in the exterior and the interior part of it.

1. The exterior part of the city-the wall and the gates, the wall for security and the gates for

entrance.

(1.) The wall for security. Heaven is a safe state; those that are there are enclosed with a wall, that separates them and secures them from all evils and enemies: now here, in the account of the wall, we observe, [1.] The height of it, which, we are told, is very high, seventy yards (Rev 21:17), sufficient both for ornament and security. [2.] The matter of it: It was as jasper; a wall all built of the most precious stones, for firmness and lustre, Rev 21:11. This city has a wall that is impregnable as well as precious. [3.] The form of it was very regular and uniform: It was four-square, the length as large as the breadth. In the new Jerusalem all shall be equal in purity and perfection. There shall be an absolute uniformity in the church triumphant, a thing wanted and wished for on earth, but not to be expected till we come to heaven. [4.] The measure of the wall (Rev 21:15, Rev 21:16): Twelve thousand furlongs each way, each side, which is forty-eight thousand furlongs in the whole compass, or fifteen hundred German miles. Here is room sufficient for all the people of God-many mansions in their Father's house. [5.] The foundation of the wall, for heaven is a city that hath her foundations (Rev 21:19); the promise and power of God, and the purchase of Christ, are the strong foundations of the church's safety and happiness. The foundations are described by their number-twelve, alluding to the twelve apostles (Rev 21:14), whose gospel doctrines are the foundations upon which the church is built, Christ himself being the chief corner-stone; and, as to the matter of these foundations, it was various and precious, set forth by twelve sorts of precious stones, denoting the variety and excellency of the doctrines of the gospel, or of the graces of the Holy Spirit, or the personal excellencies of the Lord Jesus Christ.

(2.) The gates for entrance. Heaven is not inaccessible; there is a way opened into the holiest of all; there is a free admission to all those that are sanctified; they shall not find themselves shut out. Now, as to these gates, observe, [1.] Their number-twelve gates, answering to the twelve tribes of Israel. All the true Israel of God shall have entrance into the new Jerusalem, as every tribe had into the earthly Jerusalem. [2.] Their guards which were placed upon them-twelve angels, to admit and receive the several tribes of the spiritual Israel and keep out others. [3.] The inscription on the gates-the names of the twelve tribes, to show that they have a right to the tree of life, and to enter through the gates into the city. [4.] The situation of the gates. As the city had four equal sides, answering to the four quarters of the world, east, west, north, and south, so on each side there were three gates, signifying that from all quarters of the earth there shall be some who shall get safely to heaven and be received there, and that there is as free entrance from one part of the world as from the other; for in Christ there is neither Jew nor Greek, Barbarian, Scythian, bond, nor free. Men of all nations, and languages, who believe on Christ, have by him access to God in grace here and in glory hereafter. [5.] The materials of these gates-they were all of pearls, and yet with great variety: Every gate one pearl, either one single pearl of that vast bigness, or one single sort of pearl. Christ is the pearl of great price, and he is our way to God. There is nothing magnificent enough in this world fully to set forth the glory of heaven. Could we, in the glass of a strong imagination, contemplate such a city as is here described, even as to the exterior part of it, such a wall, and such gates, how amazing, how glorious, would the prospect be! And yet this is but a faint and dim representation of what heaven is in itself.

2. The interior part of the new Jerusalem, Rev 21:22-27. We have seen its strong wall, and stately gates, and glorious guards; now we are to be led through the gates into the city itself; and

the first thing which we observe there is the street of the city, which is of pure gold, like transparent glass, Rev 21:21. The saints in heaven tread upon gold. The new Jerusalem has its several streets. There is the most exact order in heaven: every saint has his proper mansion. There is converse in heaven: the saints are then at rest, but it is not a mere passive rest; it is not a state of sleep and inactivity, but a state of delightful motion: The nations that are saved walk in the light of it. They walk with Christ in white. They have communion not only with God, but with one another; and all their steps are firm and clean. They are pure and clear as gold and transparent glass. Observe,

(1.) The temple of the new Jerusalem, which was no material temple, made with men's hands, as that of Solomon and Zerubbabel, but a temple altogether spiritual and divine; for the Lord God Almighty, and the Lamb, are the temple thereof. There the saints are above the need of ordinances, which were the means of their preparation for heaven. When the end is attained the means are no longer useful. Perfect and immediate communion with God will more than supply the place of gospel institutions.

(2.) The light of this city. Where there is no light, there can be no lustre nor pleasure. Heaven is the inheritance of the saints in light. But what is that light? There is no sun nor moon shining there, Rev 21:23. Light is sweet, and a pleasant thing it is to behold the sun. What a dismal world would this be if it were not for the light of the sun! What is there in heaven that supplies the want of it? There is no want of the light of the sun, for the glory of God lightens that city, and the Lamb is the light thereof. God in Christ will be an everlasting fountain of knowledge and joy to the saints in heaven; and, if so, there is no need of the sun or moon, any more than we here need to set up candles at noon day, when the sun shineth in its strength.

(3.) The inhabitants of this city. They are described here several ways. [1.] By their numbers-whole nations of saved souls; some out of all nations, and many out of some nations. All those multitudes who were sealed on earth are saved in heaven. [2.] By their dignity-some of the kings and princes of the earth: great kings. God will have some of all ranks and degrees of men to fill the heavenly mansions, high and low; and when the greatest kings come to heaven they will see all their former honour and glory swallowed up of this heavenly glory that so much excels. [3.] Their continual accession and entrance into this city: The gates shall never be shut. There is no night, and therefore no need of shutting up the gates. Some one or other is coming in every hour and moment, and those that are sanctified always find the gates open; they have an abundant entrance into the kingdom.

(4.) The accommodations of this city: All the glory and honour of the nations shall be brought into it. Whatever is excellent and valuable in this world shall be there enjoyed in a more refined kind, and to a far greater degree-brighter crowns, a better and more enduring substance, more sweet and satisfying feasts, a more glorious attendance, a truer sense of honour and far higher posts of honour, a more glorious temper of mind, and a form and a countenance more glorious than ever were known in this world.

(5.) The unmixed purity of all who belong to the new Jerusalem, Rev 21:27. [1.] There the saints shall have no impure thing remaining in them. In the article of death they shall be cleansed from every thing that is of a defiling nature. Now they feel a sad mixture of corruption with their graces, which hinders them in the service of God, interrupts their communion with him, and intercepts the light of his countenance; but, at their entrance into the holy of holies, they are washed in the laver of Christ's blood, and presented to the Father without spot. [2.] There the saints shall have no impure persons admitted among them. In the earthly Jerusalem there will be a mixed communion, after all the care that can be taken. Some roots of bitterness will spring up to trouble and defile Christian societies; but in the new Jerusalem there is a society perfectly pure. First, Free from such as are openly profane. There are none admitted into heaven who work abominations. In the churches on earth sometimes abominable things are done, solemn ordinances profaned and prostituted to men openly vicious, for worldly ends; but no such abominations can have place in heaven. Secondly, Free from hypocrites, such as make lies, say they are Jews, and are not, but do lie. These will creep into the churches of Christ on earth, and may lie concealed there a long time, perhaps all their days; but they cannot intrude into the new Jerusalem, which is wholly reserved for those that are called, and chosen, and faithful, who are all written, not only in the register if the visible church, but in the Lamb's book of life.

Revelation Chapter 22

Revelation

In this chapter we have, I. A further description of the heavenly state of the church (Rev 22:1-5). II. A confirmation of this and all the other visions of this book (Rev 22:6-19). III. The conclusion (Rev 22:20, Rev 22:21).

Revelation 22:1

The heavenly state which was before described as a city, and called the new Jerusalem, is here described as a paradise, alluding to the earthly paradise which was lost by the sin of the first Adam; here is another paradise restored by the second Adam. A paradise in a city, or a whole city in a paradise! In the first paradise there were only two persons to behold the beauty and taste the pleasures of it; but in this second paradise whole cities and nations shall find abundant delight and satisfaction. And here observe,

I. The river of paradise. The earthly paradise was well watered: no place can be pleasant or fruitful that is not so. This river is described, 1. By its fountain-head-the throne of God and the Lamb. All our springs of grace, comfort, and glory, are in God; and all our streams from him are through the mediation of the Lamb. 2. By its quality-pure and clear as crystal. All the streams of earthly comfort are muddy; but these are clear, salutary, and refreshing, giving life, and preserving life, to those who drink of them.

II. The tree of life, in this paradise. Such a tree there was in the earthly paradise,Gen 2:9. This far excels it. And now, as to this tree, observe, 1. The situation of it-in the midst of the street, and on either side the river; or, as might have been better rendered, in the midst between the terrace-walk and the river. This tree of life is fed by the pure waters of the river that comes from the throne of God. The presence and perfections of God furnish out all the glory and blessedness of heaven. 2. The fruitfulness of this tree. (1.) It brings forth many sorts of fruit-twelve sorts, suited to the refined taste of all the saints. (2.) It brings forth fruit at all times-yields its fruit every month. This tree is never empty, never barren; there is always fruit upon it. In heaven there is not only a variety of pure and satisfying pleasures, but a continuance of them, and always fresh. (3.) The fruit is not only pleasant, but wholesome. The presence of God in heaven is the health and happiness of the saints; there they find in him a remedy for all their former maladies, and are preserved by him in the most healthful and vigorous state.

III. The perfect freedom of this paradise from every thing that is evil (Rev 22:3): There shall be no more curse; no accursed one-katanathema, no serpent there, as there was in the earthly paradise. Here is the great excellency of this paradise. The devil has nothing to do there; he cannot draw the saints from serving God to be subject to himself, as he did our first parents, nor can he so much as disturb them in the service of God.

IV. The supreme felicity of this paradisiacal state. 1. There the saints shall see the face of God;

there they shall enjoy the beatific vision. 2. God will own them, as having his seal and name on their foreheads. 3. They shall reign with him for ever; their service shall be not only freedom but honour and dominion. 4. All this shall be with perfect knowledge and joy. They shall be full of wisdom and comfort, continually walking in the light of the Lord; and this not for a time, but for ever and ever.

Revelation 22:6

We have here a solemn ratification of the contents of this book, and particularly of this last vision (though some think it may not only refer to the whole book, but to the whole New Testament, yea, to the whole Bible, completing and confirming the canon of scripture); and here, 1. This is confirmed by the name and nature of that God who gave out these discoveries: he is the Lord God, faithful and true, and so are all his sayings. 2. By the messengers he chose, to reveal these things to the world; the holy angels showed them to holy men of God; and God would not employ his saints and angels in deceiving the world. 3. They will soon be confirmed by their accomplishment: they are things that must shortly be done; Christ will make haste, he will come quickly, and put all things out of doubt; and then those will prove the wise and happy men who have believed and kept his words. 4. By the integrity of that angel who had been the apostle's guide and interpreter in these visions; this integrity was such that he not only refused to accept religious adoration from John, but once and again reproved him for it. He who was so tender of the honour of God, and so displeased with what was a wrong to God, would never come in his name to lead the people of God into mere dreams and delusions; and it is a still further confirmation of the sincerity of this apostle that he confesses his own sin and folly, into which he had now again relapsed, and he leaves this his failing on perpetual record: this shows he was a faithful and an impartial writer. 5. By the order given to leave the book of the prophecy open, to be perused by all, that they might labour to understand it, that they might make their objections against it, and compare the prophecy with the events. God here deals freely and openly with all; he does not speak in secret, but calls every one to witness to the declarations here made, Rev 22:10. 6. By the effect this book, thus kept open, will have upon men; those that are filthy and unjust will take occasion thence to be more so, but it will confirm, strengthen, and further sanctify those that are upright with God; it will be a savour of life to some and of death to others, and so will appear to be from God, Rev 22:12. 7. It will be Christ's rule of judgment at the great day; he will dispense rewards and punishments to men according as their works agree or disagree with the word of God; and therefore that word itself must needs be faithful and true. 8. It is the word of him who is the author, finisher, and rewarder of the faith and holiness of his people, Rev 22:13, Rev 22:14. He is the first and the last, and the same from first to last, and so is his word too; and he will by this word give to his people, who conform themselves to it, a right to the tree of life, and an entrance into heaven; and this will be a full confirmation of the truth and authority of his word, since it contains the title and evidence of that confirmed state of holiness and happiness that remains for his people in heaven. 9. It is a book that condemns and excludes from heaven all wicked, unrighteous persons, and particularly those that love and make lies (Rev 22:15), and therefore can never be itself a lie. 10. It is confirmed by the testimony of Jesus, which is the Spirit of prophecy. And this Jesus, as God, is the root of David, though, as man, his offspring-a person in whom all uncreated and created excellencies meet, too great and too good to deceive his churches and the world. He is the fountain of all light, the bright and the morning star, and as such has given to his churches this morning light of prophecy, to assure them of the light of that perfect day which is approaching. 11. It is confirmed by an open and general invitation to all to come and partake of the promises and privileges of the gospel, those streams of the water of life; these are tendered to all who feel in their souls a thirst which nothing in this world can quench. 12. It is confirmed by the joint testimony of the Spirit of God, and that gracious Spirit that is in all the true members of the church of God; the Spirit and the bride join in testifying the truth and excellency of the gospel. 13. It is confirmed by a most solemn sanction, condemning and cursing all who should dare to corrupt or change the word of God, either by adding to it or taking from it, Rev 22:18, Rev 22:19. He that adds to the word of God draws down upon himself all the plagues written in this book; and he who takes any thing away from it cuts himself off from all the promises and privileges of it. This sanction is like a flaming sword, to guard the canon of the scripture from profane hands. Such a fence as this God set about the law (Deu 4:2), and the whole Old Testament (Mal 4:4), and now in the most solemn manner about the whole Bible, assuring us that it is a book of the most sacred nature, divine authority, and of the last importance, and therefore the peculiar care of the great God.

Revelation 22:20

We have now come to the conclusion of the whole, and that in three things:-

I. Christ's farewell to his church. He seems now, after he has been discovering these things to his people on earth, to take leave of them, and return to heaven; but he parts with them in great kindness, and assures them it shall not be long before he comes again to them: Behold, I come quickly. As when he ascended into heaven, after his resurrection, he parted with a promise of his gracious presence, so here he parts with a promise of a speedy return. If any say, "Where is the promise of his coming, when so many ages have passed since this was written?" let them know he is not slack to his people, but long-suffering to his enemies: his coming will be sooner than they are aware, sooner than they are prepared, sooner than they desire; and to his people it will be seasonable. The vision is for an appointed time, and will not tarry. He will come quickly; let this word be always sounding in our ear, and let us give all diligence that we may be found of him in peace, without spot and blameless.

II. The church's hearty echo to Christ's promise, 1. Declaring her firm belief of it: Amen, so it is, so it shall be. 2. Expressing her earnest desire of it: Even so, come, Lord Jesus; make hast, my beloved, and be thou like a roe, or like a young hart on the mountain of spices. Thus beats the pulse of the church, thus breathes that gracious Spirit which actuates and informs the mystical body of Christ; and we should never be satisfied till we find such a spirit breathing in us, and causing us to look for the blessed hope, and glorious appearance of the great God and our Saviour Jesus Christ. This is the language of the church of the first-born, and we should join with them, often putting ourselves in mind of his promise. What comes from heaven in a promise should be sent back to heaven in a prayer, "Come, Lord Jesus, put an end to this state of sin, sorrow, and temptation; gather thy people out of this present evil world, and take them up to heaven, that state of perfect purity, peace, and joy, and so finish thy great design, and fulfil all that word in which thou hast caused thy people to hope."

III. The apostolical benediction, which closes the whole: The grace of our Lord Jesus Christ be with you all, Amen. Here observe, 1. The Bible ends with a clear proof of the Godhead of Christ, since the Spirit of God teaches the apostle to bless his people in the name of Christ, and to beg from Christ a blessing for them, which is a proper act of adoration. 2. Nothing should be more desired by us than that the grace of Christ may be with us in this world, to prepare us for the glory of Christ in the other world. It is by his grace that we must be kept in a joyful expectation of his glory, fitted for it, and preserved to it; and his glorious appearance will be welcome and joyful to those that are partakers of his grace and favour here; and therefore to this most comprehensive prayer we should all add our hearty Amen, most earnestly thirsting after greater measures of the gracious influences of the blessed Jesus in our souls, and his gracious presence with us, till glory has perfected all his grace towards us, for he is a sun and a shield, he gives grace and glory, and no good thing will he withhold from those that walk uprightly.

Made in the USA
Monee, IL
21 October 2022

16266987R00059